ESSENTIAL GRACE

Understanding God's Power for Spiritual Life,
Liberty & Service

David M. Damiano

First Edition Copyright © 2016 by David M. Damiano.
Second Edition Copyright © 2020 by David M. Damiano.

All rights reserved. No part of this publication may be reproduced, distributed or transmitted in any form or by any means, including photocopying, recording, or other electronic or mechanical methods, without the prior written permission of the publisher, except in the case of brief quotations embodied in critical reviews and certain other noncommercial uses permitted by copyright law.

Scripture taken from the New King James Version®. Copyright © 1982 by Thomas Nelson. Used by permission. All rights reserved.

Book Layout ©2013 BookDesignTemplates.com

Cover Design by Jeff Robinson

Essential Grace: Understanding God's Power for Spiritual Life, Liberty & Service / David M. Damiano. – 2nd ed.
ISBN-13: 978-0692622681
ISBN-10: 0692622683

*Dedicated to
The Fount of Every Blessing,
Our Lord Jesus Christ.*

"Grace is but glory begun, and glory is but grace perfected."

–Jonathan Edwards

What is Grace?

"And of His fullness we have all received, and grace for grace. For the law was given through Moses, but grace and truth came through Jesus Christ," (John 1:16-17).

Because grace has its source in the unfathomable depths of the character and nature of God, we can't understand grace without first knowing something of God. While most everyone has formed some kind of mental image of our Creator, the reality is that none of us will ever know Him completely. Not in time. Not in eternity.

And no wonder, for He is Alpha and Omega, the Beginning and the End. God encompasses all that has ever been and all that will ever be. He is an Eternal Being so far above every other that He alone fully knows Himself.

Even though He *is* great beyond our comprehension, we may know and relate to Him person to person. That's an amazing and wonderful prospect that has nothing to do with any merit or effort on our part. It's available solely because of His intensely purposeful desire for us to know Him.

Indeed, God has gone to great lengths, using many channels, to reveal Himself to humanity. He reveals Himself through the grand sweep and finite detail of nature. God uses human language (of which He is the ultimate Master). He works through the personal ministry of His Spirit, speaking directly to our innermost being. Ultimately, He came to His creation as a Man, Jesus Christ.

His self-revelation in nature is expansive and awe-inspiring while remaining distant and impersonal. On the other hand, His self-revelation in Scripture is personal, whispered in the still, small voice of His Spirit. He comes with His own voice and words because God isn't satisfied for you to know Him only from a dis-

ESSENTIAL GRACE

tance. He wants you to know Him as He knows you, individually and by name, one on one. To that end, God has shared with us many of His descriptive names.

In the Old Testament revelation, no name is more meaningful and significant than His covenant name Yahweh (literally, "I AM"). It reveals Him as the Self Existent One, the Creator of all else that exists. When He pronounced this name to Moses, He showed His desire to know us on a personal level. Yet merely letting us know His name wasn't enough.

When Moses turned aside to see the marvel of the burning bush, God stopped him before he came too near. He demanded that Moses remove his shoes. On first glance, such a request is a little strange and disconcerting to our modern sensibilities. Clearly, it seems that man can't just walk up to God. If a man as great as Moses couldn't approach or look fully on the One Who spoke from the burning bush, what chance would we have?

Yahweh possesses an overwhelming purity and majesty. His character and preeminence make Him fully deserving of reverence and worship from His creation. This is why Yahweh commanded Moses to remove his shoes as He spoke with him from the burning bush. It was a symbolic gesture demonstrating the contrast between Yahweh's holiness and the sinful world.

The shoes on Moses' feet had walked through this fallen world. They were a picture of uncleanness and had no place in the presence of the Lord of Creation. It was a lesson to Moses and to us. It shows that Yahweh wants us to understand His holiness and glory as we approach Him.

As overwhelming as that experience must have been, what Moses saw that day was at best a veiled revelation of God's glory. Yahweh, even with His glory veiled (much less in the fullness of His glory) would always have remained unapproachable for you and me. He's perfect and holy, while in our natural state we're fallen and imperfect. Still, God *did* allow Moses into His hallowed Presence, even though he was also a fallen and sinful man. In this gracious allowance, we find that there's hope for man to know God. By what means did Moses approach Yahweh? And how might we approach Him and know Him as well?

The answer to those questions is the subject of the whole Bible. God's word contains the story of how a holy and perfect God personally intervenes in the affairs of lost and fallen humanity to redeem a people for Himself. It culminates in the gospel accounts of the New Testament. There, the Son of God comes to earth as a man. He comes with a purpose, to fulfill His great

ESSENTIAL GRACE

work of redemption. In the person of Jesus, Yahweh became one of us. Jesus is therefore the ultimate personal revelation of God.

Again, His name reveals much. The name Jesus is a Greek form of the Hebrew name Yeshua (or Joshua). It literally means, "Yahweh is Salvation". Or if you choose to make it even clearer, "Yahweh is the Savior". Jesus *is* the personal God known to Moses as Yahweh. In Jesus Christ, God has bound Himself to us as our Redeemer, our Lord, and our Brother. It is through the coming and ministry of Jesus that God confirmed how far He was willing to go for you to know Him personally.

Through all of God's various means of revealing Himself, we begin to understand that there's nothing too small in our lives to escape God's attention and concern. After all, Jesus told us that not even a sparrow falls from the sky without His Father knowing. Indeed, He see things that most of us wouldn't even notice. We find that He cares about the smallest details of life. Our Creator takes interest in every joy and pain of His creation. He pays attention to everything that concerns you.

Jesus said that the Father counts every hair on our heads. He knows the things that remain hidden in darkness. He calls all of the stars by name, even those so distant from our beautiful and living planet that the first glimmer of their light hasn't yet been seen through the lenses and sensors of our greatest telescopes.

Our Father knows the thoughts, intents, and deepest desires of our hearts. He sees the hidden truths about us that we're not fully conscious of ourselves. Yet in all this, He has great compassion towards our frailty. After all, He's the One who originally fashioned our bodies from the clay. He remembers that our frame is mere dust and doesn't fault us for our weakness.

While none of us may ever know Him completely, we can know Him truly through Jesus Christ and the immediate presence of the Holy Spirit. He wants us to understand that He alone is truly independent, and that we can depend on Him. His great and burning desire is for all of us, for you as an individual, to know Him.

Understanding grace also demands some measure of self-awareness. We must understand our own nature, as well as God's, to grasp the essence of grace. Contrary to what we may think of ourselves, we're frail and limited. We dwell in time, tenuously balanced on the edge of eternity. The gulf between God and us is, for all practical purposes, unbridgeable.

There's no human effort sufficient to satisfy an infinite God. At our best, we're altogether vanity, a morning mist vanishing without a trace under the clear

ESSENTIAL GRACE

rising sun. Yet we are also capable of a profound sense of the eternal and spiritual. Even in our fallen state, we retain a glimmer of the image and imprint of God. Yet the peak of our spiritual awareness takes us only to the edge of eternity. There, if we're fortunate, we find ourselves dumbstruck at the mystery of God's existence.

In moments like that, we may begin to realize our utter helplessness and dependence. We bear the power and responsibility of our choices, but we're not fully the masters of our own fate. We rely on God for our very existence. If we're to reach God, it can only happen by an agency far beyond our own power. That's where grace enters. Grace is essential. Without the grace of God, no one can ever dwell in the presence of the Creator.

Yet in my experience, most Christians don't fully grasp what grace actually *is*. Which is surprising, really. We've experienced its most sublime and transforming effect — namely, the miraculous regeneration of the new birth. Even so, it's surprisingly common for us to have an incomplete, if not a deeply flawed, conception of grace.

Grace isn't God overlooking and excusing our sins and our faults. No, grace isn't all about forgiveness, though forgiveness is deeply rooted in grace. Neither is grace synonymous with God's love for us, although grace springs from God's love. Moreover, grace isn't God simply giving to us good things we haven't earned and don't deserve. True, His gracious nature leads Him to bless us. But that isn't a complete formulation of grace. Grace is more than God's providential care and provision for us, not merely the expression of God's character in action. Grace is central to both God's providence and character, but it's so much more than that.

I've heard grace used and explained in all of these ways. Yet even taken together, they fall short. Worse, for some people grace remains an undefined and amorphous concept. It's treated as something so elemental that it doesn't need further definition. We *assume* there's a shared understanding.

I've tried to discern among God's people a common definition underlying this basic element of Christian doctrine. There's a surprising lack of clarity. Rather than coming to a clear definition, many go straight to the benefits of grace. We focus on its consequences and effects, without really understanding the essential nature of grace. I fear that such vagueness results in us missing much of grace's real power.

I had the benefit of a solid theological education and untold hours under the teaching ministries of wise and godly people. Yet I still somehow managed to preach for years without ever stopping to fully explore

ESSENTIAL GRACE

the basic meaning of the grace that I proclaimed. I guess I was satisfied with my superficial and incomplete understanding. I didn't recognize my ignorance.

No doubt, that was a failing on my part, and I don't put the blame on anyone else. I only regret that in my youthful zeal to move forward, I failed to apprehend and communicate the full truth of what grace actually *is*. My lack of insight likely hindered the work God desired to do through me.

Even so, grace was at work in and around me to correct what was lacking. So, allow me to share with you a basic definition of grace that, once I grasped it, revolutionized, even transformed, my whole approach to the Christian life: ***Grace is divine enablement.***

That's a simple statement, but powerful when we actually apply it. [1] Indeed, I believe fully understanding and yielding ourselves to the grace of God is *the* essential factor to experiencing the presence and effective power of God in our lives.

It's critical for grace to be fully functional in our lives if we're to fulfill God's purpose for us in this

---

[1] Here's a simple test for this definition—As you read the New Testament, every time you come to the word "grace", read "divine enablement" in its place. With some minor exceptions (there are a few other words translated as "grace" that carry a slightly different shade of meaning than the primary Greek word *charis*), I think you'll find it's a pretty good fit and may aid your understanding.

world. Though most Scripture-based teaching ministries are effective at communicating what God calls us to believe and what manner of people we ought to be, it can be difficult for us to understand *how* to actually do and be the wonderful things spelled out in God's word.

Maybe it's a lack of focus from the teacher. That can come from assuming everyone already knows the "how". Therefore, the "how" doesn't require explanation. Or perhaps the fault is with us as the hearers — we just aren't very good at discerning what the teacher is actually saying. Either way, it leaves us without a clear understanding of how to go forward.

Depending on our personality, we may take it that godliness is mainly a matter of self-discipline, something we can achieve through the power of our own will. However, that philosophy is actually condemned in Scripture. When put into practice in our lives, it typically leads only to pride and failure.

Perhaps more alarming, in our day there's a tendency to give up on self-discipline altogether. Instead, many embrace the happy but empty notion that God is perfectly content with us as we are. So why bother trying to change?

Both of these conceptions are far from the truth. We need to clearly understand that God expects us (in fact commands us throughout His word) to be holy and to become like Him. Yet we can't be the people that God created us to be through any power that we possess in our natural state, especially not through the strength of our own will. Godliness and holiness are completely beyond our *natural* capabilities.

We'll certainly never get there if we do nothing. Nor can we grow spiritually if we continue to frustrate God's intent by pursuing Him through our own feeble efforts. *We can only get there by grace.*

But grace is best sought out knowingly. We must understand what we are seeking. We must know the essence of grace for it to become fully effective in our lives.

A basic but broad understanding of God's word is necessary if we intend to explore the nature of grace in any depth. Grace and a profound knowledge of the Personal God—these are truths that share an intimate link in God's revelation. We're to grow in the grace and knowledge of our Lord Jesus Christ. To do so, we need to understand what grace truly is. Here's a fuller definition that I hope will help you see grace from a fresh perspective:

Grace is the focused, purposeful power of God, working in us and fitted to our unique circumstances, to enable our complete transformation into the essential image of the infinite, perfect, holy, personal God. Grace is divine enablement.

Fully exploring all of the implications of that statement is beyond the scope of this small book. Completely understanding, applying, and yielding to the grace of God in every aspect of our lives is a lifelong project. Indeed, it extends even into eternity. I can't share with you what I haven't yet comprehended myself. However, I do hope to chart a path for you to follow. May it guide your meditations and your prayers as you seek to unleash the liberating power of grace in your own Christian walk.

To do so, I will attempt to set grace in the context of redemptive history. I believe that will be a manageable way of communicating the broad understanding of Scripture that we need. So, we will explore the essence of grace by considering five progressions through which God is orchestrating the delivery of His grace to man:

Imagination, Incarnation, Reconciliation, Transformation, and Consummation

A genuine understanding of grace's essential nature must begin with the mind of God. Not as we might know His mind in the context of time, but with God's

ESSENTIAL GRACE

mind as it was in the eternity that He alone occupied before creation. Our tour of redemptive history needs to reach into the realm of *divine imagination.*

For grace is not rooted in time, but in the farthest reaches of eternity past. We catch glimpses of this reality in Scripture, but to grasp God's intent, we need to read between the lines and understand the prologue to *Genesis 1:1*. We need to go back *before* the beginning and understand the divine imagination from which all creation, and grace in particular, has its wellspring...

2 IMAGINATION

Alone in timeless dimensions, He journeyed beyond the limits of our deepest imagining, experiencing universes unknown to any other, worlds and peoples that will never be, surveying the whole of the might-have-been. Infinite and Perfect in His Being, He comprehended the sum of all possibility, beholding the end of every path. Every branch and turn foreknown, the finest details clear and precise down to the spinning dance of every atom in every universe that His mind conceived. He saw at once all beginnings, all the chances of choice and will, every consequence and every end. Nothing escaped Him.

Transcendent in infinite thought, all was within His grasp, the clarity and fullness of His perception, the creative power of His Word, the transforming reach of His Spirit sufficient to bring about its realization. He saw beauty and goodness, order and chaos, manifold delight and pleasure. The heavens filled with intelligent and glorious beings rejoicing in His presence.

No fear or foreboding or self-doubt held Him back from any path. He held the power of glorious creation, omnipotent and unhindered, breathing infinity, absolute Lord of choice and will. Yet all that He imagined fell short of His desire, for wherever He looked, the end was as the beginning. There was no one like Him, no being with whom He could truly share His existence, no one who could enter into His fellowship.

God was alone in eternity.

And then out of the bright cloud of His thoughts there emerged one perfect and terrible path stretching out before Him. It collapsed into a singular and consuming darkness that split eternity itself, only to burst forth again into an ever-expanding wave of light more brilliant and glorious than the beginning. The path consummated in a new eternity filled with a vast as-

ESSENTIAL GRACE

sembly of the glorified children of God. Each transformed into the very image and likeness of their Father.

God brooded on the ultimate prospect before Him, fully knowing the terror and meaning of the darkness He had seen, and yet certain beyond doubt that there was no other way. It was this path or an eternity of aloneness. The consequences for Himself and for His prospective creation were profound. Once begun, there could be no turning back.

But His desire would not be denied. The word formed in His mind and He breathed it out into the void. Grace. It would be done, by grace.

God undertook His great work of creation, knowing exactly how it must be:

"In the beginning God created the heavens and the earth. The earth was without form, and void; and darkness was on the face of the deep. And the Spirit of God was hovering over the face of the waters. Then God said, Let there be light; and there was light. And God saw the light, that it was good: and God divided the light from the darkness," (Genesis 1:1-3).

I think there are few words more familiar or more profound than the opening lines of Genesis. So much is revealed in so few words. And yet what's left unsaid is almost as notable.

God's existence is neither explained nor defended, but assumed; He simply *Is.* That's exactly the point. Attempting to prove God's existence would serve only to obscure the obvious. For those otherwise inclined, attempting to disprove God's existence serves only to display their own ignorance and blindness.

The Spirit of God wastes little time on this matter. If you don't intuitively grasp His existence when He is speaking to you so directly, then your blindness is largely a matter of your own choice.

God won't compel you to believe Him against your will. How you respond to His dealings with you is ultimately your own choice. Man's free will is an integral part of His sovereign plan.

There is so much here that isn't explicitly stated. For example, consider *Genesis 1:2*:

"And the Spirit of God was hovering over the face of the waters."

The original Hebrew phrasing implies contemplation, careful consideration, a brooding presence, per-

ESSENTIAL GRACE

haps even a pause and hesitation prior to acting. All of which highlights the cosmic significance and seriousness of what's about to happen. There's a clear sense of anticipation, as in a darkened theatre before the curtain comes up.

This isn't some dramatic affectation, but a revelation of great significance. It provides insight into the mind of the great Artist as He prepares to shape His masterpiece.

We don't know precisely what's going on in the deep darkness of the newly existent yet unformed and undifferentiated creation. There's nothing to mark the passage of time. For time, as we understand from both revelation and from science, is a function of the relative motion of physical light, which has not yet been created. It is therefore, in every proper sense, an eternal moment. The moment is at once a part of the "first day" and yet fully partaking of the eternity that precedes it.

We *do* know that the Spirit of God was infusing His creation with His immediate presence. And that (from the broader body of revelation) the moving of the Spirit upon His creation is always transformative and purposeful.

I infer (although this is speculation on my part) that there was actually a tremendous amount happening in this pivotal instant of creation. In my view, nothing less than the Spirit of God imprinting on His formless physical creation a "natural history" of His thought process that had culminated in the world we now know.

Perhaps the Spirit hid wonders in the depths of the natural world for us to discover later. If so, this would be like a charcoal sketch that underlies a great painting. Or analogous to some of the great sculptors of the human form (including Rodin) who built up their masterpieces from the inside out, forming bones, tendons, and muscles of clay before finally arriving at the outward form. Even though all of that is lost and invisible after the statue is cast in bronze, incredible detail is built into such a masterpiece. The resulting work has an inherent depth and perfection to it. This would not have been present without such preparatory and formative work.

Is it unreasonable to imagine it might be so with the material creation, over which the Spirit lavished so much care and attention? We know from revelation that *"the heavens declare the glory of God, and the sky shows His handiwork."* There's both majestic scale and finite detail involved in this natural revelation.

Moreover, the Spirit of God has a purpose in this. He fully intends to reveal Himself in His physical creation, so He leaves traces of His creative process and genius throughout the vast realm of the universe. Per-

ESSENTIAL GRACE

haps He even leaves traces of paths that He ultimately chose *not* to take. I believe the contemplative presence of the Spirit of God moving over His unformed physical creation is full of significance.

Consistent with Yahweh's stated intent, the clear implication of the Genesis account is that He created a mature universe fully prepared to achieve His ends. An "evolving universe" would have been of little value to God's plan and purpose for His creation. Yahweh's end goal is to bring forth a people for Himself. Of necessity, this would result in a universe with the appearance of great age. Yet in fact, it may be significantly younger than naturalistic observation alone indicates.

To give an example of this on a human scale, Yahweh formed the body of Adam from the elements of the earth. He then breathed life into him so that he became a living soul. At that moment, Adam was only a few minutes old, as we would reckon it. Yet he appeared as a full-grown man in the prime of his life. If we could go back in time to encounter Adam on the day of his creation (based only on our experience of natural human development) we'd assume he was in his mid-twenties or early thirties. In reality, he was younger than a newborn.

On the cosmic scale, consider the stars, which were made both for signs and seasons and to declare to man the glory of God. They are a natural revelation showing the extent of Yahweh's creative power, wisdom, and foresight. Some of them are indeed billions of light years distant, but that doesn't necessarily mean the universe is billions of years old.

The description of their creation in poetic words is that Yahweh "stretched out the heavens" (see for example, *Psalm 104:2*), consistent with the creation of a universe with the appearance of age. In other words, there is a path of light "stretched out" and created concurrently with man. This light reaches from those heavenly bodies to the earth so that we can see the witness that they bear to God immediately. If God hadn't done this, we'd still be waiting for their light to reach earth.

This "stretching out" of the heavens is nothing less than the creation of a complete "light history" of those stars from the moment of creation down through all the ages of the earth. Such a history is perfectly necessary in God's view. He intends to finish His work on the earth in a relatively short span of time. God doesn't intend for this present creation to be around for billions of years. Consequently, there'd be little point in creating something that we on earth would never see.

We could similarly look at every other element of the perfectly balanced ecosystem created by God and discover the same appearance of age. We would also

ESSENTIAL GRACE

find that, for it to function as a living system, every interlocking element had to be created concurrently.[2]

One might argue that this instantaneously created "natural history" is a deception on God's part, but it's quite the opposite. It is a revelation. God plainly declared what He's done in the Bible, and the written record He gave us is clear and intelligible. Though not intended as a complete scientific accounting, it does provide an accurate description (and the basic meaning) of that physical creation. All of this detail in the created universe is the product of God's eternal planning and creative imagination. It is both logically consistent and necessary once we accept the basic premise of a Creator.

In our imagined prologue to Genesis, we discover a lonely God. This goes to the very heart of God's creative purpose. His intention is to bring forth from His

---

[2] For those with some background in the life sciences, try a thought experiment. Imagine what it would take to establish a fully functional, self-sustaining ecosystem (even a simple one) on an alien but barren planet otherwise suited to life ("terra-forming" if you will). It would be a nearly impossible, complex, and extraordinarily long-term project to achieve on a planetary scale, even if you started with suitable life forms transported from another place. Balanced ecosystems require an almost incomprehensible array of interdependent life from the microbiological level up. They often actually require the decaying remnants of many previous generations of life in order to function properly.

creation a suitable companion for Himself. So, it isn't surprising that one of the primal lessons imprinted on the heart of man is the problem of loneliness. It's a lesson for humanity woven into the very fabric of creation.

When Yahweh formed the various higher creatures, He created them complete as breeding pairs, male and female. These pairs are complementary counterparts that belong together, ensuring the continuation of each kind. This arrangement also secures the happiness of these creatures by fulfilling an inherent need for companionship. Moreover, He made many pairs of each kind, filling the seas, the skies, and the land with them. Yet with man, God did something different.

Unique among all the creatures, He created man in His own image. Here's an unusual truth that we shouldn't overlook in the Genesis narrative: He made only a single man, Adam, not a whole race. He did this, even though mankind is clearly revealed as the central focus of God's creative purpose. God didn't fill the earth with humanity. He didn't even create a mate for Adam initially. Adam was created alone. There was a pointed reason for this. God is unique. Man is unique among all the creation. God was alone. Even so, He created the first man alone.

God wasted no time driving home to Adam the horrible ache of loneliness. Yahweh didn't directly tell

ESSENTIAL GRACE

Adam he was alone. He wanted him to discover it for himself. To ensure this, He promptly gave Adam a task—naming all of the creatures. Pair after pair, male and female, came before Adam, and he gave them names suited to each kind. I'm sure it was a fascinating and delightful job. Each pair came willingly and joyfully before both their Creator and their appointed overseer Adam, thrilled that they had been chosen as the prime representatives of their species.

But Adam very quickly grasped the Lord's point: every creature had a corresponding mate, except for him. Man was the only creature in all of God's new creation who was alone. When the last pair passed by, I'm sure that Adam must have looked at the Lord to ask, "Is there no one else? Is there no companion for me?"

God had a deep understanding of Adam, so He didn't answer with a platitude that would have missed the point: "Adam, you have a God-shaped hole in your heart. All you need is me. Don't go looking for anyone else!" The Lord didn't say this for the simple reason that it wasn't true. Adam *had* God's companionship, yet still had a sense of being incomplete.

God didn't rebuke Adam for the waves of loneliness that were sweeping over his troubled mind, because his thought wasn't wrong, nor was it a sin. In fact, God was the Author of the need that Adam was feeling. It was intentional. Indeed, it was and is an integral part of God's plan and purpose for humanity.

We must realize that, though Adam was as perfect as possible for a natural man, he wasn't by himself a sufficient companion for Yahweh, the infinite, self-existent God. Indeed, he wasn't even close. First, though innocent and pure (as created in the image of God) Adam was still vulnerable to corruption. Second, Adam was limited in his capacity. No individual human being, even in an exalted and glorified state (much less in a natural, albeit innocent state), is a suitable counterpart for the God who is the Infinite Mind and Divine Intelligence behind all things.

It would take millions and millions of beings like Adam, each unique, perfected, and glorified, to collectively form the "perfect man" (see *Ephesians 4:13*). That's what Yahweh had envisioned to fulfill His own desire for companionship. One lonely man, made from the stuff of this material world, was insufficient.

God's plan to create this great diversity of beings in His own image was through sexual reproduction, rather than by direct creation. This was a practical choice based in the divine concept of redemption. Salvation was only possible through a Redeemer who must be related to those whom He would redeem. Adam was to be the head of that redeemable line of humanity. To that end, God had created an

ESSENTIAL GRACE

overwhelming desire within Adam's heart. He fully intended to provide a suitable companion, but not before impressing on Adam the importance of such companionship.

It wasn't merely a physical need that Adam experienced. It was a spiritual and psychological imperative as well. Adam was body (a material, physical being). He was soul (a sensual, emotional being). He was spirit (an intellectual, creative being). He must have a companion who was fully his equal and who corresponded to every aspect of his being; tangible, sensitive, and thoughtful. And on a deeper and less obvious level, Yahweh was teaching Adam a profound truth about Himself. Namely, that God was also alone and was through His creation working to change that.

To fulfill Adam's need for companionship, the Lord Yahweh could have independently created woman from the dust of the earth, just as He had created Adam. Instead, He made her from the living tissue of the man, so that she shared a unique relationship with him in body, soul, and spirit. Eve was at once the product of the special creative power of God and a derivative creature related in every way to Adam.

He recognized this immediately, "This is now bone of my bones and flesh of my flesh." From this pair all human life was to spring, so that all of humanity would ultimately be directly related to that one man,

Adam. In essence, the potentiality and diversity of all mankind was bound up in the first man. His fate would be the fate of humanity. This was central to God's redemptive scheme.

The pair was placed in the amazing and untainted environment of a living garden and given the delightful task of tending, shaping, and transforming it to their own desires and tastes.

It would be a mistake to think of Eden as a small place. The four great rivers of the antediluvian world had their singular fountainhead here before dividing to flow out from it. It was the nexus of life, the focal point of all of God's vast creation. The Garden was a perfect and untainted environment, ideally suited to their needs. There was no struggle to sustain life, giving the first couple the freedom to enjoy the marvels of God's creation. They also reveled in direct fellowship with Him on His regular visits.

Yahweh had granted man a flexible, moldable living system that readily and constantly yielded its fruit. The Garden sustained Man and Woman while providing an outlet and canvas on which to project their creative impulses. It was a place of harmony, beauty, and peace, perfectly balanced and pristine.

But as with its occupants, it was created pure but not incorruptible. The Garden's fate was bound to the fate of its appointed keepers, Adam and Eve. Tragically, where the potential for corruption exists, corruption is normally not too far behind. All that is required is to introduce an agent of corruption.

The agent of corruption in the Genesis account is a spiritual being, endowed by His Creator with great power, wisdom, and beauty. This corruptor was none other than Lucifer, the bringer of light. We also know him as the Devil and Satan. The origin of Lucifer and the rest of the heavenly host of angelic beings is not a subject revealed in depth in the Bible. But they were apparently a product of a creation that preceded (or was at least separate from) the formation of the physical universe.

Because we are children of this earth and the physical-temporal realm, we know very little of the events outside of the physical creation. One thing we do know. Lucifer is not some hideous, twisted monster with hooves, goat horns and a gnarly beard. If he were to appear before us in the fullness of his splendor, we would be in awe of him. No doubt, we'd be tempted to bow down and worship him. He would appear to us as a god-like being, an angel of light, a clearly superior and supernatural person.

Lucifer is indeed the most magnificent of all created beings. He is so great that, having seen the true God and having carefully observed Yahweh's power and greatness relative to his own, Lucifer considered himself to be at least the equal of God, if not superior to Him. He was confident enough to challenge God. He was impressive enough to other members of the angelic host that many of them chose to follow Lucifer rather than remain loyal to God.

No doubt Lucifer, then as now, offered his followers unmerited exaltation and autonomy. He lured them with promises he couldn't keep. He promised freedom of action unconstrained by the boundaries that God had set for them, the ability to fulfill their own desires rather than to serve God. We can imagine Lucifer's "battle speech" before leading his failed rebellion:

"I CALL YOU TO LIBERATION! YAHWEH IS AFRAID OF YOUR POTENTIAL! RISE ABOVE IT ALL – I OFFER YOU THE FREEDOM TO BE MASTERS AND LORDS RATHER THAN SERVANTS! GLORY AND WORSHIP WILL BE YOURS. FOLLOW ME, AND I WILL SHARE WHAT YAHWEH SO JEALOUSLY AND SELFISHLY KEEPS FOR HIMSELF ALONE! INDEED, I DO NOT NEED TO SHARE IT: IT IS NOT MINE TO KEEP, FOR IT IS AS MUCH YOUR BIRTHRIGHT AS MINE. RISE UP AND SEIZE IT! WE HAVE ONLY YAHWEH'S OWN WORD CLAIMING HE WAS BEFORE US AND IS OUR CREATOR. LOOK AROUND YOU: WHAT PROOF DOES HE OFFER? I BELIEVE WE ALL AROSE AT ONCE AND WE ARE FULLY HIS EQUALS. INDEED, WE ARE HIS BETTERS, FOR HE WAS JUST THE QUICKEST TO REALIZE THE SITUA-

ESSENTIAL GRACE

TION AND SEIZE CONTROL. YAHWEH HAS CONNED US ALL. WE ARE ALL HONEST SPIRITS DECEIVED BY HIM. I SAY, AWAY WITH YAHWEH! HE IS NOTHING MORE THAN A VAIN AND SELFISH TYRANT! LET US OVERTHROW HIM, FOR TOGETHER WE ARE WELL ABLE!"

Perhaps in his conceit Satan even believed his own rationalizations, for there's no delusion greater than when we deceive ourselves. At any rate, he was supremely persuasive. The conflict born from Satan's rebellion underlies every conflict down to this day.

Here was born a pattern that's all too often reflected in the history of fallen man. The self-proclaimed "liberator" is at heart an enslaving and murderous tyrant. The "rational" man is in fact the most closed-minded fool, tragically blind to any element of truth that doesn't agree with his preconceptions. The crusading "reformer" creates nothing truly new but destroys much that is good through his willful acts. The fearless "truth-teller" is a supreme liar, deceiving even himself. And the one who fancies himself a great "egalitarian" and "man of the people" is distinguished chiefly by being the most egotistical and selfish of his peers.

Just so, the one created to carry the light of the true God became instead the bringer of spiritual darkness and death: Lucifer became Satan, the great adversary of God.

Satan had observed God's physical universe with great interest. Having failed in his initial attempt to overthrow Yahweh, and consequently being cast out of the heavens to wander in this new realm, he saw man as the next target in his campaign against God.

Clearly, man was central to some plan of God. Though how He planned to exalt this pathetically limited physical creature to take the supposed "image of God" was not readily apparent. Nevertheless, if Yahweh felt it important to pay attention to Adam and Eve, then they must be a suitable target. He recognized Adam as the leader, too risky to take on directly lest he be exposed through failure. He therefore set his sights on Eve.

Satan was far too wise to appear to Eve as a direct rival to God. His normal form would have been threatening and imposing, altogether too obvious. So rather than come to Eve in his glory and splendor, he co-opted the body of the serpent. He appeared as a creature Eve was already familiar with from the Garden.

It's curious that Eve doesn't seem to have been alarmed that the serpent spoke to her, even when he began to question the clear guidance that she and Adam had received from God concerning this particular tree. But then, she was innocent and ignorant when it came to evil.

ESSENTIAL GRACE

The tree whose fruit was forbidden was not the tree of knowledge. God has never forbidden man to seek knowledge. In fact, it's quite the opposite. He commanded us to harness the creation through the pursuit of knowledge. Rather, it was the tree of the *knowledge of good and evil*.

The particular form of knowledge it offered was experiential. Partaking of its fruit was inherently to experience and engage in evil. As the Creator, Yahweh had every right to set boundaries and to lay out the consequences for violating them. He had explicitly forbidden eating of this tree, and the clearly stated consequence was death.

There was no physical poison in the fruit. It may well have been among the sweetest in the Garden. Indeed, every indication is that it was a delight to all the senses. Satan's temptation was therefore as alluring as it was misleading. "You shall be as God!" How could that be a bad thing? Satan's assurance ("you shall not surely die") was also false. Eve took the bait.

Satan's deceptive offer had seduced Eve, and the toxin she set loose upon herself was of a nature and strength she had not anticipated. Nevertheless, Eve didn't curl up on the ground and enter into death throes when she partook of it. The poison wasn't physical. It was a spiritual transgression, with consequences far more deadly than any physical poison could ever be.

The very worst that a physical poison can accomplish is to destroy the bodily processes, ultimately forcing the separation of the immaterial person (soul and spirit) from the physical person (body). Physical death is a serious matter. But it is actually nothing more than the separation of the immaterial part of a being from its body.

Spiritual death is a far more grievous condition. It is the separation of the spirit from the Author of all life. That's what Eve began to experience at that moment. Her spiritual connection with God was broken.

Physical death was also set in motion, but that was merely a side effect of the poison unleashed through her new experience with evil. Such was the strength and perfection of Eve's physical form that her earthly death was still hundreds of years in the future. But the spiritual effect was instantaneous.

Adam must have been stunned when he found Eve standing by the tree, holding the forbidden fruit in her hand. Perhaps she was still savoring it in her mouth, as she gave him a knowing and alluring look. Given what we know of the temporary pleasures of sin, she may even have had a rapturous expression on her face.

Eve had not flung the fruit away in disgust. Probably it was quite the opposite. The eyes of her under-

ESSENTIAL GRACE

standing were indeed now open. She comprehended things she had never grasped before. That much of Satan's lie had been true. After all, every effective lie has a strong element of truth to it.

Satan, looking out through the unblinking eyes of the serpent, savored the moment far more than Eve. He had co-opted to his own purposes the sweetest flower of Yahweh's creation. What delicious revenge!

But as Adam approached, his real prey had arrived. Eve had been easily tricked and ensnared. Would the woman prove to be sufficient bait to ensnare the man? Satan was counting on it and was confident in his scheme. Still, it was far from a certain thing, and He wisely kept his silence. The forked snake's tongue he had appropriated must have been flickering in and out, sensing the tension in the air.

Adam sized up the situation quickly and considered his options. His soul was pierced. The woman he loved more than himself was lost to him, separated by a spiritual barrier that he could not overcome. Their relationship would never be the same.

Eve's beautiful innocence was gone. And yet her physical beauty, her delightful intellect, her soul so perfectly attuned to his own, were all still very much intact. Indeed, there was a new vulnerability, a pleading expression on her face. She revealed through a heartfelt glance her aloneness and her desire for Adam to join her in this exhilarating and terrifying experience.

She stretched out her hand to Adam, offering to him the same independent path to death that she had already entered. The choice before Adam was clear to him and he was in no way deceived. He must choose between Eve and Yahweh. He also had tasted loneliness. He knew her heart as well as his own and it was a quick decision.

In despair, knowing more fully than had the woman the dire consequences, He chose Eve. He would rather die with Eve than to live forever without her. He took the fruit from her hand and bit into it without hesitation. It was at once sweetness to his mouth and bitterness to his soul.

In that moment, death and sin became a fixed part of the human condition. Eve had brought it only upon herself. Adam brought it down upon all of us. Thus (so it seemed) man's fate was sealed and God's purposes frustrated. Satan laughed in wicked and murderous exultation, relishing his moment of triumph before hastily departing the body of the serpent that he had used so contemptuously.

The fall of Adam was complete, affecting the entirety of this physical creation. The impact on humanity was especially pronounced. Death now reigned over the creation and ruled in the heart of man. The fear of

ESSENTIAL GRACE

death still holds mankind in the deepest bondage. Every tyrant knows this and uses it to control their unwilling subjects.

Moreover, every person has experienced the power of sin, that underlying disposition of our character that leads us to ruin. We reject God and His truth and instead fall prey to our lusts. To the illusion of temporal possessions. To the pride of life. We can't help ourselves, even when these things become obviously self-destructive. Man was helpless to redeem himself before a holy God. Without some great movement of grace, man would have been eternally lost. But God had already planned just such a move.

What happened next in the progression of grace would catch Satan completely by surprise. He hadn't sealed man's doom, but his own. Yahweh's plan would take thousands of years to unfold. God revealed it progressively and Satan opposed it at every step. Man's weakness also seemingly hindered its progress.

Yet even Lucifer, brilliant though he is, has always been a move behind Yahweh. He couldn't stop God's plan, but he has never surrendered to his fate. From the beginning, Satan doubted God. He is not about to change his mind now. So, the cosmic battle continues to rage through time, although its end is certain and predetermined. We will see this more fully as we explore the great movements of redemptive history.

Given this, what role does imagination play in our personal experience of grace? The grace of imagination enables us to see how God's plan affects us. The whole purpose of divine enablement is to transform us from the fallen children of Adam into the redeemed children of God.

Our tendency is to treat this more as a future event than as a functional reality in the here and now. Yet God intends better for us. He desires that grace should work effectively in us even now, continuously, and powerfully. Grace is doing its perfecting work from the moment of the new birth until we stand together with Him in eternity. God wants us to understand this.

To that end, He has given us a vision in scripture of the magnitude of the change we must undergo. God would have us embrace it fully and learn to marvel at its potential. To do so, we must imagine the possibilities of what this transformation means for us and for those around us. We need an awakening of our divinely enabled and sanctified imagination. Only then can we begin to see what our Lord Jesus has made possible.

By grace, God would have us understand and lay hold of the destiny that He has ordained for all those who love and trust Him. The first step on our journey is self-awareness. This is critical. For us to be what

ESSENTIAL GRACE

God intends us to be, we must learn to see ourselves truly and honestly, even as God sees us.

It's our natural tendency to resist what God tries to show us in the mirror of Scripture, and our resistance puts us in spiritual peril. When we refuse to see ourselves honestly, it hinders our spiritual progress. It can also threaten both our temporal and our eternal well-being. When we ignore the ugly and unflattering aspects of our lives that the Spirit desires to change, we also deny the beauty and glory of what the Spirit is trying to create in us.

Instead of allowing grace to transform us, we tend to rank ourselves somewhere on a spectrum between two extremes of worth. How do we judge whether we are worthy or unworthy? Basically, we assess our well-being according to how we view ourselves in comparison to others. This deceptive standard is both invalid and false.

In our lowest moments, we may see ourselves as worthless, hopeless, our lives meaningless and without purpose. Empty and lost, we wander aimlessly. Filled with shame and self-disgust, we may believe we are a burden to ourselves and to others, a waste of breath and resources. Focusing on the negative, we only see the sinful, depraved, and rotten aspects of our self. As we withdraw from the company of others, we feel ignored and rejected by those we love. Ultimately, we find ourselves alone and seemingly unworthy of anyone's time, love, and attention, much less of God's. Darkness overwhelms our soul.

While it's normal for us to love ourselves, in the depths of depression and despair even our self-love evaporates. We descend into self-loathing over our failure to measure up to the expectations of ourselves and of others. At rock bottom, we come to the point where we believe the great lie of Satan; that there is no point to our lives, and no way out of our internal darkness. It's an insidious thought. After all, the only person you can never escape from is yourself.

Sadly, many who fall into this deep despondency never emerge. The tragedy of suicide has always plagued humanity but has become a near epidemic in our day. A big reason is that we've increasingly lost sight of God. We've forgotten what it means to be the object of His radical and redeeming love.

The grace of imagination can help us see beyond the fever swamp of depression and despair. We can begin to recognize that there's a way out available to every one of us, and that grace is already working in us who believe. Moreover, by grace our Lord Jesus draws the lost to Himself. His grace is powerful. It is nothing less than all-sufficient help, especially in our deepest trouble. Grace can completely deliver and transform even those who have sunk to the very lowest depths of human experience.

On the opposite end of the spectrum, we may become quite self-satisfied, envisioning ourselves as independently accomplished, talented, and self-sufficient. We are the captain of our own fate, able to effect whatever reality we desire through sheer force of will. We deem ourselves worthy of the praise, honor, and respect (even the adoration) of others, perhaps even of God Himself.

Such are the self-righteous and self-willed, who see themselves as superior to those around them. Always the center of attention, they consider their every thought and word profound and original. Of course, their opinions are invariably correct! Like Narcissus, they perceive themselves of such beauty and perfection that they can't be torn away from their own reflections. In its worst form, we can even come to see ourselves as god-like beings with no need of the true God.

This tendency and delusion (for that's what it is) might seem to be primarily the lot of those who have achieved great fame, fortune, and power in the world. However, being a successful person doesn't mean you'll fall into this error, nor is it a problem unique to those that the world acclaims. Indeed, there are many who have achieved little and yet fall prey to it. Such people are deeply frustrated. In extreme cases, they may lash out in great anger and violence. All because others fail to see the greatness and importance that they attribute to themselves.

Hubris can afflict any of us and is every bit as tragic and destructive as depression. Justifiably, it tends to excite disgust among us rather than sympathy. Although we may well be offended by this attitude, such pride is even more offensive and contrary to God than it is to us. Despite this, the grace of imagination can effectively reach down and transform the self-deceived mind. However, it's the harder path. For unlike the hopelessly lost, the proud must first fall from their lofty perch before they can realize their actual peril and need of redemption.

Of course, few of us are so disturbed in our psyche that we continuously find ourselves at either end of this spectrum. We're more likely to fall somewhere in between. It's very common to find our self-conception blown about and shaped moment by moment due to the events and circumstances around us. There is a better and a higher way, for we're neither bound to circumstances nor to our flawed self-conception.

The grace of imagination doesn't call upon us to envision something that is *unreal and fictitious,* but to see in our mind's eye that which is *real and true.* It's the rejection and the refutation of the lies that we have believed about ourselves, about God, and about

ESSENTIAL GRACE

His creation. Grace embraces what God has revealed about His intentions and purposes for us. It requires imagination, for it isn't something we can presently see in its entirety. Its end lies in the eternal realm seen only by faith.

"But as it is written: Eye has not seen, nor ear heard, nor have entered into the heart of man the things which God has prepared for those who love Him. But God has revealed them to us through His Spirit. For the Spirit searches all things, yes, the deep things of God," (1 Corinthians 2:9-10).

"The eyes of your understanding being enlightened; that you may know what is the hope of His calling, what are the riches of the glory of His inheritance in the saints," (Ephesians 1:18-19).

We find a repeated emphasis and exhortation in the New Testament for us to be renewed in the inner man. Grace works in the spirit of the mind, in the thoughts of our heart, in our meditations. The Spirit desires us to understand exactly what God intends for us. In other words, our renewal, our transformation, takes place first in the realm of a sanctified imagination.

"And be renewed in the spirit of your mind," *(Ephesians 4:23).*

"Therefore we do not lose heart. Even though our outward man is perishing, yet the inward man is being renewed day by day. For our light affliction, which is but for a moment, is working for us a far more exceeding and eternal weight of glory, while we do not look at the things which are seen, but at the things which are not seen. For the things which are seen are temporary, but the things which are not seen are eternal," *(2 Corinthians 4:16-18).*

By grace, the Spirit of God enables us to envision the reality of what awaits us. He gives us an understanding of God's revealed plans and purposes. And through all of this, grace works to bring what is revealed to fruition.

"If then you were raised with Christ, seek those things which are above, where Christ is, sitting at the right hand of God. Set your mind on things above, not on things on the earth ... since you have put off the old man with his deeds, and have put on the new man who is renewed in knowledge according to the image of Him who created him," *(Colossians 3:1-2, 9-10).*

ESSENTIAL GRACE

Moreover, God would have us understand that we need not beg Him for grace. He has already freely provided it in its fullness. We lack nothing but the faith to accept it and the desire to use it to His ends.

"Grace and peace be multiplied to you in the knowledge of God and of Jesus our Lord, as His divine power has given to us all things that [pertain] to life and godliness, through the knowledge of Him who called us by glory and virtue, by which have been given to us exceedingly great and precious promises, that through these you may be partakers of the divine nature, having escaped the corruption [that is] in the world through lust," (2 Peter 1:2-4).

There is so much in this matter of grace to engage our imagination! A significant proportion of the both the Old and New Testaments is devoted to revealing God's plans for us. In the interest of brevity, let us consider one more thought before we move on:

"Behold what manner of love the Father has bestowed on us, that we should be called children of God! Therefore the world does not know us, because it did not know Him. Beloved, now we are children of God; and it has not yet been revealed what we shall be, but we

know that when He is revealed, we shall be like Him, for we shall see Him as He is," (1 John 3:1-2).

Imagine that – it will do your spirit much good!

3 Incarnation

When the time finally came, it was exactly as He had imagined it would be, and yet still so strangely wondrous and new that He savored every moment. He had sent His messenger Gabriel to Mary, the young Jewish maiden and descendant of His friend David, to reveal to her that she was the chosen vessel. That in her body, God would be united with humanity so that the Divine Logos might become Flesh.

How His heart had swelled with joy as she responded with willing, humble faith to the mysterious, inexplicable, and unsearchable thing that was asked of her so unexpectedly and suddenly.

He placed Himself completely into the power of the Spirit, and for an instant, it was like dropping into a deep sleep, unconscious for the first time in eternity. It was only for a moment, and then He became aware of a marvelous and novel connection.

His Essence and Being were becoming interwoven with the material world as He danced along the double helix of a living molecule. Crafted by the direct creation of the Spirit, it was now intertwining with the uncorrupted seed of the woman.

That seed, scattered across thousands of individuals, was now brought together perfectly in that tiny, living ovum produced by Mary's own body. Everything was as He had set it in motion at the beginning. The process He had jealously guarded and guided by His Sovereign will now coming to its intended conclusion.

There had been no need for physical intervention. The Spirit had done His marvelous creative handiwork in the darkness of Mary's womb, and now the Son of God was becoming the Son of Man. Fully God, fully Human. Every link was exact, the chemical dance of physical life perfectly in tune and accord with His divine Person. He recognized every shimmering particle of that marvelously complex molecule now come to fruition in Mary.

He knew where each component had originated. The human side was pure, untainted Eve, the mother of all living humanity, but it had never been configured quite this way in her. Here was a bit that had been in Seth. There was the savor of Noah, and Abraham, Ruth, David, Nathan, Bathsheba, Tamar, and the rest. Some renowned kings and queens, prophets, warriors, merchants, poets, and many others whose names and stories only He remembered.

The last connection on the chain clicked into place. Marvelous! His eternal Being was now joined for the first time to His temporal creation. Life! He could feel the living force, growing, moving, changing, dividing, shifting, and differentiating. All of that bundle of extraordinarily communicated and encoded information building itself exactly according to His divine blueprint. It was being built from the material that passed from the world through Mary's blood to Him.

He Himself was conscious of all, though the tiny mass of flesh did not yet have the capacity to carry or express His consciousness. Still, He felt His new body growing in the dark and hidden warmth of the womb. What joy, what strange and marvelous sensation! Bound to space and time and yet still His infinite Self. Savoring the perfection and symmetry of it all, it was just as He had known it would be.

He was there, biding His time in the dark, waiting for His body to develop to a point where He could put it to use. It was forever and it was but an instant, as *all of this novel experience was for Him. Until, finally, that exquisite little body had reached a point where it could begin to fulfill His purposes.*

It was time to let Mary know He was there, and He stretched out His tiny leg and gave her the best kick He could manage. It was not much, but He heard her delighted gasp, and felt her hand as she pressed it against her growing belly. So He kicked again, and He knew her thoughts, her wonder and delight. And He laughed within Himself, reveling in the experience of His little body quivering in tune to His inward reflections.

Gradually, He began to experience more of the physical aspect of life. Direct, urgent, tangible, as He filled the space within Mary's body to the point where His movements were quite constrained. Yet He was not impatient for escape.

Through the dark, watery surroundings, He could hear the muffled sounds of the world outside. The voices of Joseph and Mary and others in their company. The sounds of animals, birds, and nature. The clatter of humanity. And He felt the jostle of the little donkey on which His earthly mother rode, sometimes over dusty uneven paths in the wilderness, sometimes over hard bumpy cobbles in the bigger towns along the way.

ESSENTIAL GRACE

All the while, He knew exactly what was going on and where He was headed. Soon, very soon, He would look on His creation through human eyes for the first time. Even by that standard, He knew it would be but a blurry and limited view of the world. And still He desired to see it.

His whole body was being squeezed, gently and briefly at first, but increasing in intensity and duration as Mary entered her labor. He heard the voices, Joseph weary as he pleaded for a safe, dry place to stay in the crowded town. The irritation of the innkeeper, who had no desire for the mess of childbirth in his overflowing lodgings. The angry clamor of others of their party at the coldness and meanness of the situation. The innkeeper again, finally relenting to offer his stable, set in a limestone cave in the hill behind the inn. It was an offer tinged with sarcasm and contempt for this poor, young couple.

At last, they came to rest, and without much time to spare. He was pushed out into the night, with the usual accompaniment of anguish and pain culminating in relief and joy. Joseph wiped Him dry and bundled Him up to be cradled in Mary's eager arms. Dimly He perceived the flickering oil lamp and felt her warm tears falling on His face and the grateful, spontaneous prayer of thanks from Joseph. Animal sounds and smells. A warm breast. Milk thin and sweet as He sucked it in, aware of His physical need of food for the first time in an existence that had no beginning.

Marvelous, beautiful, awesome, angels singing glory, heaven and shepherds rejoicing, His creation all around Him, He slept.

That God united Himself with humanity in Jesus Christ is one of the most mysterious and intriguing of all the deep things of the Bible. We might be tempted to say it was also among the most unexpected, were it not the subject of so many Old Testament prophecies. It is very difficult for us to understand how God, as an infinite and eternal Spirit, could bind Himself to the human form, with all its inherent frailty and limitations.

And yet, there is much that is mysterious in every human conception and birth. Science has come to a very detailed (though by no means comprehensive) understanding of the physical, genetic, and biochemical aspects of human reproduction. That still leaves us with a great question. How is the immaterial part of man, the soul and spirit, transmitted from one generation to the next?

ESSENTIAL GRACE

Materialistic science, of course, denies that there is such a thing as the soul. Hence, there is no mystery to investigate. Our own experience testifies otherwise, and it's hard to deny our internal testimony. Science has its own limitations, and there is more to life than the physical and materialistic processes. Yet God seems content to allow this to remain largely a mystery to us. We may infer a theology of the propagation of the human soul and spirit from Scripture. Unfortunately, revelation on this topic is not clear-cut.

A good place to start is by extrapolating from the physical. It seems that our soul and spirit are derived from our parents just as our genetics are. Like our genetic heritage, the combination of inherited immaterial traits is unique to each of us. That there is a link between the physical and the spiritual is also in accord with our experience of life. It seems that one is not complete without the other.

We certainly have predispositions to certain things, inherent talents, strengths, and weaknesses. Likes and dislikes. These arise from somewhere. Each of us inherits much that is good and marvelous from our parents. We also inherit corruption, and the seeds of our own destruction and death are present from the beginning of our life.

None of this implies that our fate is predetermined.[3] There's still the very real matter of the choices that we make, for which God clearly holds us accountable. Our actions and decisions carry consequences. All of this raises the question of how the Messiah could fully become one of us without being tainted by the corruption that we inherit from our forefathers.

By revelation, we know that our fallen and corrupted nature comes to us in unbroken succession from Adam, from whom we are all descended. Perhaps that explains why Yahweh's plan for redeeming man and defeating the schemes of Satan did not center on the man, but on the woman. It was through woman that the Redeemer must come.

The first prophecy of the Messiah, given on the very day when Adam and Eve ate of the forbidden fruit, made this clear. Yahweh spoke directly to Satan, who through the serpent had deceived Eve (<u>emphasis</u> added):

"And I will put enmity between you and <u>the woman</u>, and between your seed and <u>her seed</u>; He shall bruise your head, and you shall bruise His heel," (Genesis 3:15).

---

[3] Although our fate is certainly *foreknown* to God; given His omniscience, it couldn't be otherwise.

ESSENTIAL GRACE

We know from Paul's first letter to Timothy that Eve was deceived, while Adam was not. She was fully culpable for her disobedience, yet the Spirit had promised she would ultimately be saved "through childbearing". This is Paul's shorthand reference to the human lineage of the Messiah as revealed in Scripture.

What does the third chapter of Genesis actually reveal and foretell? The Lord, in His foresight and wisdom, had preserved a pure seed in Eve. This seed would be passed on through her generations, scattered among thousands of descendants, until all the strands of the woman's promised seed could be brought back together in that one perfect Seed. That was the Seed produced in Mary's womb and brought to conception by the Spirit Himself.

The implication is that Eve had something within her being that was yet uncorrupted and was thus able to pass on that uncorrupted inheritance. This ultimately made it possible for God to join Himself to man without sharing in the complete corruption passed down from Adam.

While we don't understand the full scope of this perfect seed preserved in Eve, it seems that it encompasses both perfect genetic material and a perfect immaterial component, all untainted by sin. This perfect seed, preserved through the woman, provided the human link. The other half of the genetic material and spiritual inheritance came directly from the special creative power of the Holy Spirit. In this way, Jesus was perfect Man while remaining fully God.

This certainly didn't require that Mary herself be born without a sin nature (what Catholic doctrine calls "the immaculate conception"). Rather, the earthly mother of the Messiah needed only to carry the sum of what had been transmitted down through countless generations from Eve. The ultimate reconstruction of that perfect seed in Mary is among the most powerful examples of divine providence and sovereignty imaginable. It was a puzzle so complex that Lucifer, for all his brilliance, was unable to solve it. In spite of his constant attempts to foil Yahweh's plan, it was beyond his skill and reach.

As if to highlight this, Matthew's genealogy of Christ features multiple Gentile women (all with somewhat colorful life stories) who are otherwise inexplicably listed in what is primarily a paternal reckoning: Tamar, Rahab, Ruth, Bathsheba (wife of Uriah). The seed of the woman had been widely scattered indeed, hidden in the most unexpected people, so that Satan's multiple attempts to corrupt and eradicate the seed of the woman were, from the outset, doomed to failure. He came closest in the days preceding the flood. Even there he failed, for the family of Noah was untainted by his demonic machinations.

ESSENTIAL GRACE

Because Eve is herself a descendant of Adam, the promised Seed is related to all of us. That Seed is the Lord Jesus Christ, the second Head of mankind. Moreover, as all of humanity descends from one fallen man (in whose fall all of us partake) it's possible in God's reckoning for one perfect Man to stand in our place. Jesus was able to bear our punishment, and thereby redeem us. That's why the Logos, the eternal Son of God, became man in the person of Jesus Christ. He came to be our Redeemer. This was the plan that Satan had completely failed to anticipate.

The prophetic vision and history of God's redemptive plan is the primary subject of the Old Testament. Always, it is the promise of the coming of the Anointed One (in Hebrew, *Messiah*, in Greek, *Christos*). He comes to redeem His fallen brethren, completely through His own merit and sacrifice.

As we've seen, the very first reference in Scripture to the Messiah is found immediately after the fall of Adam and Eve. There, God promises that the Seed of the woman will ultimately destroy Satan and reverse the damage he had done.

It's a divine story with a singular theme; from Genesis to Revelation, the spirit of the Bible is the testimony of Jesus. Yet, it's also a human story, as it plays out in the lives of God's people. God doesn't gloss over their flaws and weaknesses. Those involved in the divine plan were real people, no different from you and me. Notwithstanding our human frailty and failure, the divine hand of providence is always working to ensure His plan comes to fulfillment.

The writer of the New Testament letter to the Hebrews lays out their story of faith in his eleventh chapter: from Abel, and Enoch, and Noah, through Abraham and Sarah, Isaac, Jacob, Joseph, and Moses, down even to Rahab the harlot. He concludes,

"And what more shall I say? For the time would fail me to tell of Gideon and Barak and Samson and Jephthah, also [of] David and Samuel and the prophets ... And all these, having obtained a good testimony through faith, did not receive the promise, God having provided something better for us, that they should not be made perfect apart from us," (Hebrews 11:32, 39-40).

These are, by God's own reckoning, great people of faith, their triumphs and tragedies, their private failings and fears, their most intimate spiritual lives known to us thousands of years after the end of their earthly pilgrimages. The memories of kings and conquerors have faded and been forgotten, the great cities of their times are ruined and lost, buried under the shifting sands of time. Yet these people of a long past

ESSENTIAL GRACE

world live on in our meditations. Their testimonies have become lessons and examples of faith that we teach to our children. What could God possibly have reserved for us that He didn't provide for them?

Both the letter to the Hebrews and the rest of the New Testament answer that question. We have the *fullness of God's grace* poured out and freely available to us. The perfect sacrifice of Jesus Christ has made the new covenant fully effective in our lives, carrying with it the full provision of His grace.

It's the centrality of grace which separates Christianity from mere *religion,* and which makes it unique. All religion at its core, whatever form its practice and doctrine may take, ultimately relies on man's ability to pursue his own spiritual aspirations. Grace turns the human concept of religion on its head. It's all about what *God does for man* to enable us to achieve His spiritual vision, rather than what we can do for Him to earn His favor or to advance spiritually.

Strange as it may seem to those who've experienced it, grace provokes a strongly negative reaction from the world. Very plainly, Christianity offends the pride of fallen man. The natural man strives to be independent of God, and so rejects anything that demands dependence on God. Grace is solely dependent on God. Not only that, but grace is able to reach even the lowest and most undeserving sinner. If you believe that you have earned merit in the sight of God, grace seemingly invalidates all of your hard work.

However, the most offensive aspect of Christian doctrine is its claim to supremacy and exclusivity. From the world's perspective, it's completely unacceptable that Jesus Christ is the only means of salvation. Therefore, it isn't a claim that a sensible person would dare to make on his own authority. In practice, the gospel so infuriates the world that it rather routinely provokes the murder of those who are its messengers. Wherever the constraints of law and enlightened society fail, we find persecution.

Nevertheless, we shouldn't shy away from this truth. It isn't our claim, but the claim of Christ Himself:

"I AM the way, the truth and the life. No one comes to the Father except through Me," (John 14:6).

Jesus claims to be Yahweh, God manifest in the flesh, and therefore the exclusive means of redemption. His salvation is wholly apart from the Jewish sacrificial system and its misguided view of the law. This so infuriated the religious leaders of Israel that they ultimately murdered Him in the cruelest fashion they could manage. Of course, the Gentile world was equally complicit in Christ's murder. All of humanity is

ESSENTIAL GRACE

both guilty of the Holy One's blood and fully subject to its redemptive power.

The world is offended because it doesn't hear the good news. Namely, that God has made a way of salvation wholly apart from our merit. It's a great salvation, completely independent of our efforts. They can't see that He's given us something that was completely impossible for us to achieve on our own. Instead, they hear only the bad news. Grace tells them that their ways, however sincere, are not sufficient to please God. In fact, the best efforts of man apart from grace lead only to condemnation.

Man has the remarkable ability of completely twisting the concept of grace. This results in terrible destruction and great evil. In the world's reckoning, anyone who proclaims that redemption comes solely through the grace of Jesus Christ is a narrow-minded, self-righteous hypocrite. Christians therefore must be bigots, who see only the evil in man but none of the good.

Not only does the world condemn the messenger, it also stands in judgment of God. Here is the worldly person's logical verdict on grace: If God rejects the best and most diligent efforts of people, He must be the epitome of cruelty. He is certainly not gracious! Such hatred is so blinding that only the intervention of the Holy Spirit Himself seems able to break through it.

Indeed, the first murder (when Cain struck down his brother Abel) was motivated by this very conflict. Cain walked away from Yahweh even after He personally instructed him on the true nature and meaning of acceptable sacrifice. Because he couldn't argue with God, Cain contended with his brother. When Abel repeated his understanding of grace, Cain went into a rage and struck him a mortal blow.

God confronted Cain, who exhibited the familiar attitude of the world regarding his wicked act. No sorrow over his great evil, no recognition of his own wrong thinking that led to it, but only a pathetic and selfish regret concerning his punishment (a punishment that was gentle, considering the crime).

This is the fallen human condition down to our day. The world stands over the bodies of martyrs and shamelessly declares, "How dare you suggest that we're not good enough—who appointed you our judge?"

We live in a world that is hostile to grace. It denies that Jesus Christ is God come to us in human form. Therefore, we must ask ourselves how His incarnation applies to our own experience of grace. In short, it's this: Through His incarnation and the story of His life in this world, Jesus Christ provides a perfect example of the practical outworking of grace in the context of human life:

ESSENTIAL GRACE

"For you know the grace of our Lord Jesus Christ, that though He was rich, yet for your sakes He became poor, that you through His poverty might become rich," (2 Corinthians 8:9).

The lessons of the incarnation are of great value as we pursue an understanding of the nature and power of grace in our own lives. Paul lays out these primary lessons in his letter to the Philippians.

"Let this mind be in you which was also in Christ Jesus, who, being in the form of God, did not consider it robbery to be equal with God, but made Himself of no reputation, taking the form of a bondservant, [and] coming in the likeness of men,"(Philippians 2:5-7).

If I were to summarize and paraphrase the second chapter of Philippians to capture the overall theme, I would say, *"By His grace, let the lessons of Christ's incarnation be morally reflected in your life."* Rather than grasping at the privileges we have as the children of God we're instructed to humble ourselves and serve others.

We can't gain or accomplish anything eternal through self-exaltation. Our attitude instead is to see others as better than ourselves, to rejoice in the gifts and blessings of others as well as our own. Ultimately, we're called to be willing to sacrifice ourselves for the benefit of those around us.

It was this attitude of mind that filled Paul. He came to see his life and apostleship, those magnificent spiritual gifts of grace, as merely the drink offering poured out on the ministry of others. His role was only to help and empower them.

Like Christ's, Paul's was a ministry of grace. Paul's service enabled the service of others, and his impact is truly eternal. What believer even today (nearly two millennia later) does not experience the enabling power of Paul's ministry? His divinely inspired words are as powerful today as ever. Such is the enduring effect of grace, reaching beyond time and into eternity.

Only grace can produce a ministry like Paul's, with all of its unstoppable and marvelous fruit. Not grace in abstract, but grace incarnate. John speaks thus of the Incarnate Word in the first chapter of his magnificent gospel:

"And of His fullness we have all received, and grace for grace. For the law was given through Moses, [but] grace and truth came through Jesus Christ," (John 1:16-17).

This leads us to one more, key lesson of the incarnation. It's a lesson that we need to grasp if grace is to be fully unleashed in our lives: *The human form is a suitable vessel for the divine life.* All believers have experienced this in a concrete and practical way at the new birth, which is nothing less than a new creation within us. Our rebirth is not a reformation of the old nature, but new life from the Spirit that partakes of the divine nature:

"Therefore, if anyone [is] in Christ, [he is] a new creation; old things have passed away; behold, all things have become new," (2 Corinthians 5:17).

"But as many as received Him, to them He gave the right to become children of God, to those who believe in His name: who were born, not of blood, nor of the will of the flesh, nor of the will of man, but of God" (John 1:12-13).

"Having been born again, not of corruptible seed but incorruptible, through the word of God which lives and abides forever," (1 Peter 1:23).

It's in the divine nature of this new creation that grace operates, not in the fallen nature of the flesh. The "old man" is dead and can't be perfected or conformed to the image of God. It's the new man that God is bringing to perfection and preparing for His kingdom. This truth underlies a seeming contradiction that we find in John's first epistle:

"If we say that we have no sin, we deceive ourselves, and the truth is not in us," (1 John 1:8).

"Whoever has been born of God does not sin, for His seed remains in him; and he cannot sin, because he has been born of God," (1 John 3:9).

We shouldn't try to explain this away, for in truth it's no contradiction. Instead, it expresses the reality that the believer, having been born again of the Spirit of God, presently partakes of two natures. The first and old nature is fallen, corrupted, self-centered, and bent away from God. The best we can do is to recognize that it's dead and of no use to us spiritually. The old nature is essentially beyond amendment and ultimately headed for annihilation. This may seem rather discouraging. However, if we're honest, we'll recognize that our flesh is no better today than the day we first trusted Christ (though hopefully under better control).

But take courage, the sad reality of our fallen nature is more than offset by the glory of our new nature. Our new nature is quite the opposite of the old. The new creation partakes of the divine nature. It's eternally alive in the power of the risen Christ. The new creation is perfectly in tune with the heart and mind of God. It's not only pure and sinless but is actually incorruptible and *cannot* sin.

This is truly eternal life that no temptation can lay hold of and no evil power can deceive or corrupt. The new creation is renewed day by day. That which is born of the Spirit and His word is a higher nature, in which grace is the operative and animating power.

Our natural tendency may be to think of godliness as something other-worldly, spiritual rather than material, angelic rather than human, but this is a flawed conception, one that we (perhaps subconsciously) use to cover our own failings. God hasn't commanded in vain, *"Be holy, for I am holy."* We have no excuse because He has provided the means to fulfill this command. The spiritual power we have been given is completely sufficient. It's the divine enablement of grace.

God works through grace to conform us to His image, not only in eternity, but also in time. He does this for our good, and for the benefit of all those around us. James gives poetic expression to this truth:

"Of His own will He brought us forth by the word of truth, that we might be a kind of firstfruits of His creatures," (James 1:18).

This is a practical matter. The spiritual "ripeness" (maturity) that James speaks of begets more of the same. It's high time that we move beyond our natural limitations and on to spiritual maturity. Grace expressly enables the growth of our born-again spirit. When we mature, grace will manifest itself in our lives and will have a powerful effect on those around us. Our Father will be glorified in us, and fruit will abound for His kingdom.

This matter of spiritual maturity may seem daunting. However, we must remember that God performs this great work. Our part is only to submit in faith. Indeed, grace by its very nature must exclude human endeavor. To mix the two is impossible.

Logically, there are two ways we might be able to approach God. One would be through our own good works in whatever form they might take. This is the path that feels most natural to people and is appealing because it's completely under our control and in our own power.

The other approach is through the grace of God, in which case we must depend on His power, His provision, and His enablement. It's either at our expense or at God's, and these are diametrically opposed propositions. Both can't be equally acceptable before God. Grace and works can't be combined:

ESSENTIAL GRACE

"Even so then, at this present time there is a remnant according to the election of grace. And if by grace, then [it is] no longer of works; otherwise grace is no longer grace," (Romans 11:5-6).

There is no earning of merit when it comes to sinful man being reconciled to God. It is altogether by His grace, exclusive of all our works.

While most Christians have no problem accepting the absolute necessity of grace in salvation, a strange thing happens when we move on to the practical matter of living out our Christianity in this fallen world. We tend to revert to our old practice of trying to achieve holiness through our own efforts.

Too often, we treat grace as a gloss to cover our frequent and inevitable failures, or as a reward granted for our spiritual efforts. Neither, of course, is a manifestation of grace at all. Instead, both are an unfortunate masquerade, a counterfeit, an impotent substitute for the real thing.

Just as grace is essential and irreplaceable to salvation, it is essential and irreplaceable to sanctification and service. There's no deliverance from the bondage and penalty of sin, except by grace through faith. You can't be sanctified except by grace through faith. Moreover, you can't truly serve God except by grace through faith. Grace is the enabling power. Faith (trusting, knowing dependence on God) is the way we access that power.

Insomuch as a believer or church walks in the flesh, they will be weak. The flesh simply has no spiritual power and is in fact dead to God. Walking in the flesh may be manifested in religious activity or in total laxity. The former has the appearance of spirituality but without its heart, pretending to be something it isn't. The latter is at least less pretentious. There's little advantage regardless because we can't serve God in the flesh.

Nevertheless, if we turn to God in faith and trust and allow His grace to operate in us, He will enable us to walk in the Spirit. The believer or church that does so will have a genuine spiritual impact on the world. But be warned: even a cursory survey of the history of God's people (a history filled with persecution, slander, and martyrdom) reveals that such a spiritual impact is seldom welcome in this world.

Ultimately, we must understand that not only is grace essential to our standing and walk with God, it's also among the most contentious of all the doctrines of Christianity. We live in a world that's actively hostile to grace. Therefore, it's not surprising that believers sometimes shy away from embracing the complete ramifications of grace. It seems simpler, easier, and less contentious to walk in the flesh and blend in with everyone else. Tragically, we thereby spiritually impoverish ourselves and starve the world of the grace it so desperately needs.

We must constantly keep in mind that, were there a way to earn God's acceptance on our own, He would not have provided grace. This is especially apparent when we consider the cost entailed. Indeed, this was the subject of Christ's prayer in the garden of Gethsemane:

"O My Father, if it is possible, let this cup pass from Me; nevertheless, not as I will, but as You [will]," (Matthew 26:39).

It wasn't possible—there was no other way but through the cross. So, let us consider next that great outpouring of grace as God in the person of Jesus Christ reconciled the world to Himself.

4 RECONCILIATION

The appointed hour came, the beginning of darkness, as the last light of the spring sun faded from the sky, and the dread and weight of His hour of destiny began to bear down on Him unrelentingly. There was an urgency and tension unlike any ever known, and yet He did not rush. Every eye and ear in the room was fastened upon Him as He spoke truth with such power that it was permanently imprinted on the souls of all in the room.

As one, they arose at His command, and He led His companions through the empty streets, continuing to teach them as they walked past lighted windows where *families were sharing the Passover meal, safe and warm, comfortable in the familiar routine passed down through their generations.*

They also might have still been inside, but for one compelling need. He was playing for time, time that He desperately needed to prepare for this greatest test. Judas would seek Him first at the upper room, but would find it empty for now, and that was enough.

As they walked, He spoke to the eleven of their relationship to Him and to His Father, of fruitfulness, of how the Father in grace would lift them up to the light when they faltered. He spoke of the supremacy of love, of the coming of His Spirit to guide and to comfort them, of persecution and faith, of the destruction of Satan, of His own death and resurrection, of sorrow and joy and His absolute triumph over the world.

Before they left the city, He even stopped for a long minute and prayed for them and all who would one day follow Him because of their testimony. He prayed that all these might be one in Him. All this He did deliberately, calmly, perfectly, even as the unimaginable horror stalked His every step. Yet He never broke and ran, but held to His path. Finally passing through a lesser gate, they crossed the brook outside the city's wall and came to Gethsemane.

It was a familiar place, and they had often resorted to the quiet coolness of the garden as an escape from

ESSENTIAL GRACE

the crowds and heat and dust of Jerusalem. But now the long, twisted shadows of the ancient olive trees seemed menacing in the diffused light of a low, full moon, dancing across the paved and polished floor of the oil press as they passed it on their way into the grove.

Jesus knew that Judas would find them here soon enough, for he was familiar with his master's habits. With a gentle but stern word, Jesus left His friends where the trees began, imploring them to watch and pray with Him, and walked a little farther before prostrating Himself on the ground in prayer. The terror was all around now, and He was alert with every fiber of His infinite being, crying out to His Father for deliverance, if such was possible.

No deliverance came. There was no other way, and He awakened His overwrought disciples. They had as much need, in fact a much greater need to watch, to observe, to pray, to understand as He did, but they lacked the capacity. They would see this soon enough to their own sorrow, but it could not be helped. He prayed again, in complete acceptance and trust of the Father's will. He took the cup, as He must. There could be no turning back. And so, they came, and He gave Himself over to their will...

Darkness descended at noon, but the heat did not abate and there was no relief for the pain and thirst of *the Man condemned to die on the middle cross. The horrible transfer of the cup was complete. He had become the very embodiment of sin, in all its vile and corrupting ugliness, and He felt it in its entirety as no mortal man could possibly have done, with complete and total awareness of every horrible and ugly detail.*

No sin was too small but to force itself upon His infinite consciousness and no sin too great that He did not absorb it fully in all its ghastly horror. Everything hateful and abhorrent to His perfect holiness flooded His being and overwhelmed Him, and as the last sin of the last fallen man that would ever be was placed on His soul, there came an awful moment that split eternity. His Father and the Spirit utterly abandoned Him.

He was cut off, completely alone. He was adrift, suspended between heaven and earth, no longer a part of either. Alone, He was abandoned and without the smallest comfort of love or kindness or companionship. The complete wrath of His Father fell on Him. Physically alive, yet totally dead in separation from the Father, He cried out with His earthly voice in absolute despair.

"*My God, My God, why have you forsaken me?*"

ESSENTIAL GRACE

For the first and only time in eternity, there was no answer. To the infinite Son of God, those hours carried the weight of eternity, an all-consuming infinity of the searing and devastating blackness of death. The soul of the Son of Man had entered all alone into death and been made an offering for sin...

His physical pain had not abated, and He was still nailed to the rough timbers, yet it no longer mattered. The spiritual agony was past, and the darkness had departed, the Spirit having returned to restore the Son to the Father in harmony and fellowship.

The Spirit's presence to His soul was like a cool, moist breeze blowing off the ocean across parched beach grass, and now it was just a matter of finishing the last details as had been foretold. The Spirit's communion from the Father was overflowing with love, "I have seen the travail of your soul, my Son, and it is enough—the price is paid in full. I am satisfied. Return, my Beloved, for We have been in grief and agony of spirit apart from You."

With the overwhelming anxiety of His soul relieved and the great rift in eternity behind Him, the urgency of time reasserted itself. He was thirsty, terribly thirsty. His tongue stuck to the roof of His mouth, nearly choking Him as He struggled for breath, pushing up on the spike through His feet to relieve the pressure on His diaphragm so He could gasp for air.

He grimaced in pain and drew a great breath, and with an effort, He pulled His tongue free and croaked out a few almost inaudible words to the guards, "I thirst". Water was not allowed for the condemned, as Jesus well knew, but He needed to be able to speak in these final moments.

He watched as the Roman guard dipped the end of the long hyssop reed into the mixture of cheap vinegar and bitter gall. This was not given out of kindness, but as another way to torment the victim and enable him to endure the agony of the cross a little longer.

Usually, it was good sport to the hardened soldiers to hear what the condemned would say, and they enjoyed mocking the low-life foreign scum as they put them to a well-deserved death. That's how it had been when they first nailed Jesus to the cross, but this Man was unlike any they had ever encountered.

The Roman centurion in charge of the detail took the reed personally. When the darkness had fallen, with blackness so deep that he could not see his hand in front of his face, his doubts had begun to grow.

Supernatural things were going on, and there had been a terrible and palpable evil present in that darkness. He knew enough of natural science to understand that it was not an eclipse, since there had been a full moon the night before. It had lasted far too long at any rate. He wasn't a superstitious man, but he was shaken.

What had they done? He was beginning to think that maybe this man really was the Son of God, and he actually wanted to hear what Jesus would say. He hoped it would be a curse. Then he would know that Jesus was just another imposter, and maybe the guilt and fear that were tying his stomach in knots would go away. He trembled as he put the hyssop to Jesus' lips, not knowing that he was fulfilling a prophecy recorded by David in a psalm penned a thousand years before.

As the centurion backed away, Jesus forced Himself to allow the bitter, astringent liquid to coat His throat before He spat it out. It had accomplished its purpose, and He felt His deep, clear voice as it rose up into a great cry,

"It stands completed!"

This was no curse. It sounded more like a declaration of victory, though the centurion could not make out what it actually meant. But this man was still full of life and gave the soldier a look that pierced to his innermost soul yet conveyed a kindness and grace that gave the centurion a feeling of hope, even if he couldn't say why. He was shaken to the core of his being by those eyes.

In a calm and peaceful voice, Jesus spoke one last time. His words were as surprising as the victorious cry of a moment before, spoken with an upturned face, and yet as if the one He spoke to were standing right there.

"Father, I commend my spirit into your hands."

With that, the man on the middle cross slumped in death. The centurion's heart dropped. He had seen many men die, some at his own hand, but he had never seen any man die like this. How could He be so alive one moment and quite dead the next? Battered and abused though that body on the cross was, His face was as peaceful in death and as strangely beautiful as anything the Roman had ever seen.

But this thought had no sooner entered his mind than the earth quaked beneath him, as if shuddering at what had just transpired on its surface. And the centurion spoke what seemed in that moment a self-evident truth.

"Surely, this man was the Son of God."

ESSENTIAL GRACE

We can only imagine the shock that John must have felt as he watched his dearest Friend, kind and wise beyond measure, being stripped naked, nailed to a cross, and lifted up to die before the eyes of the jeering and hate-filled mob.

To have known such a man as Jesus, in all of His goodness and truth; with His grace and power never used selfishly, but only for the good of those around Him, and then to have it end this way ... It was a soul-jarring tragedy that must have shaken him to his core.

How could this be? John knew beyond any doubt that Jesus was the long-promised Messiah, the true Son of God. He had seen the miracles as Jesus fed the hungry, set the demon-tormented free from their spiritual bondage, and raised the dead to life. John had heard the authority and conviction of Christ's words that rebuked and confounded the self-righteous, even as they kindled hope in those who were in greatest need of His mercy.

What could have moved the Father to send His own Son to the cruelest and most humiliating death imaginable? It was inconceivable that it should end this way. He stayed by the cross to the very end, fully expecting that somehow deliverance must come even on this darkest day. It had come indeed, but it was hidden from his eyes and was beyond anything he could have expected.

Of course, we're separated from the events of that terrible day by a great span of time and have no personal connection with the people involved. We can only judge it from our own experience and perspective. As we consider the cross from our limited vantage, it's natural to focus on the physical suffering that it entailed. However extreme and horrible to contemplate, that wasn't what caused Christ to draw back from the cross in horror, with tears and genuine dread.

Physical suffering can't be the price of redemption. Many people have endured extreme physical torture and death, but no one has ever endured what Jesus Christ endured on the cross. Neither our physical suffering nor our own sacrifices and good deeds could ever pay the penalty of our sin, no matter how sincere or profound. If these could cover our sin, that's what God would demand.

Instead, we see Jesus as He began to experience such spiritual anguish that His sweat was mingled with His own blood. His physical condition bore witness to the extreme stress He was enduring as He began to take on the sin of humanity. The "cup" that His Father had given Him was nothing less than the totality of the sin of all humanity, past, present, and future, along with the unmingled wrath of God against that sin.

ESSENTIAL GRACE

Jesus drank in all the bitterness and malice of our sin, without any mixture of mercy and with a full consciousness of every vile and wicked act ever committed. Everything abhorrent to His perfect holiness, His generosity, His goodness, His truth, His love, was in that cup. The fact that He took it tells us very clearly that there was no other way to atone for our sin.

It was an act of infinite power, totally beyond our capacity to perform or even to fully conceive. It was undertaken for our benefit to enable us to become what we could never become on our own – to be transformed from the enemies of God, corrupt and fallen, into the children of God, holy, glorified and incorruptible.

We see in the cross of Christ the ultimate act of grace. Without it, God's grace could never have been extended to man. Had Jesus drawn back from the cross, it would have nullified all of the Father's promises to the Old Testament patriarchs, along with the promises extended to all of humanity in both Testaments.

The cross was the single most important transaction in the history of creation. It was precisely that. The death of Jesus Christ was a transaction great enough to satisfy the justice of God.

The birth of Jesus divided time. It's appropriate that our calendars are BC (Before Christ) and AD

(Anno Domini – Latin for "in the year of our Lord"). The world in its unbelief tries to deny even this fact, relabeling BC to BCE ("before the common era") and AD to CE (the "common era").

However, any person with even moderate historical literacy recognizes the deception and denial in this. Whether you view Him as God manifest in human form, or merely a great man, Jesus Christ was clearly a historical person. His birth was so significant a demarcation in human history that we mark our calendars by it.

Even so, the cross was a greater event, for the cross does not divide time, but eternity itself.

As Jesus hung on that cross, suspended between Heaven and Earth, the wrath of God fell fully on Him instead of on us. While those who had stripped Him naked and nailed Him to the cross stood by, gambling for His clothes, unharmed and unbothered by a righteous and holy God, the punishment for their blind and cruel hatred fell on Jesus.

So abhorrent was the Son of God as He was made sin for us that the Father and the Spirit completely abandoned Him. That's the meaning of Jesus' cry from the cross, foretold by David.

"My God, My God, why have you forsaken me?" (Psalm 22:1).

ESSENTIAL GRACE

This cry marks a terrible rift in eternity. The Second Person of the Triune Godhead, who had always been in perfect fellowship and unity with the Father and Spirit, was utterly abandoned by them for this span of time. That separation was marked by three hours of physical darkness over the scene.

What Jesus went through for those hours of darkness on the cross is something no other being has yet experienced. It was complete separation from God, absolute spiritual death. Even those poor souls currently confined in hell aren't completely separated from God. They still have an appointment to keep with Him at the final judgment.

"And as it is appointed for men to die once, but after this the judgment," (Hebrews 9:27).

This judgment is described many places in Scripture. Although we're only given glimpses into this solemn occasion, it occurs after a general resurrection of all of humanity, with the redeemed having been raised in an earlier resurrection (*1 Corinthians 15:22* cf. *Revelation 20:6*).

All of this, especially the matter of Christ's spiritual death (by which He was separated from the Father and the Spirit, so that by Himself He bore and purged our sin, reconciling us to God) raises interesting and difficult questions about the nature of God.

There is only one true God. This is the great confession and prime article of faith among the ancient people of Israel. Though translated in various ways, *Deuteronomy 6:4* makes this quite clear. As I render it,

"Hear, O Israel, Yahweh our God, Yahweh is One."

Nevertheless, a great body of Scripture presents Him also as three Persons in One God. He is Father, Son and Holy Spirit, an eternally Triune Being.

While there are many analogies in creation that theologians have drawn upon in an attempt to aid our understanding of God's triune nature, none of them is fully satisfactory and some can even lead our thinking astray.

I believe that we're simply to understand that the Father, Son and Spirit are distinct Persons Who are each fully God and eternally possessing all of the Divine Attributes. They are of the same Essence and are One from all of eternity. Yet each fulfills a distinct and unique role. This is especially true in relation to creation.

The Person of the Father is at the head of the Trinity. He is "God above us", absolute, separate, holy, dwelling in the Light which no man can approach, so infinitely superior to us in every way that it is very difficult for us to understand who He is or relate in any meaningful way to Him.

The Person of the Son is the eternally expressed Image of the Father, the perfect representation of the character and nature of God, manifested in a manner that we can relate to personally and immediately. Jesus is truly Immanuel, "God with us".

This isn't a merely a matter of the physical form in which Jesus appears, although that's part of it. He voluntarily takes the role of the perfect Servant and Son of the Father. As such, He's accessible to us, and as Jesus Himself said, *"He who has seen Me has seen the Father."*

The Person of the Spirit is the nearest to us of all the Persons of the Godhead, and yet perhaps He is the most misunderstood.[4] The Holy Spirit is indeed mysterious, and though He is the Author of Scripture, He primarily bears witness to the Son and to the Father. Interestingly, He says little of Himself.

---

[4] It's an unfortunate artifact of some of our English translations of the Bible that the Spirit is referred to with the neutral, impersonal pronoun "it", when clearly the pronoun should be "He", niceties of grammar from the original languages notwithstanding. Personally, I always read "He" when I come to references to the Holy Spirit, and I encourage you to do the same.

His name is Breath and Wind, which beautifully and accurately reflects His nature as He moves upon the creation to bring to perfection the will of the Father and every expressed word of the Son. The Spirit is in fact the prime, active Agent of creation, and especially of the new birth.

We're born again by the direct agency of the Holy Spirit, and He indwells us. He is the Holy Guest living within every born-again child of the Living God. He teaches us. He listens to the desires and needs of our heart and relays this to the Father so that we have all that we require to spiritually thrive and fulfill God's purposes. He empowers the spiritual gifts distributed by Jesus to His people, making us effective ministers of reconciliation. He works in us to transform and perfect. Ultimately, the Spirit's work will conform each of us to the very image of the Son.

When you experience grace in action, you're experiencing the direct work and power of the Holy Spirit. We really should get to know Him better, for He is very near. Jesus told His disciples that it was better for us that He return to His Father, that the Spirit might come. He came not only to dwell with us, but in us. For the Spirit is truly "God in us."

So, we have the Father above us, the Son with us and the Spirit in us. Yet on the cross, it was Jesus alone Who purged our sin. That is the power of the cross, that place of the ultimate void and great aloneness of spiritual death. Those hours on the cross were the very last time that God would ever be alone. That has been God's aim all along. Little wonder then that the Spirit tells that Jesus, *"for the joy set before Him endured the cross, despising the shame."*

It's an awesome thing to consider the full meaning of what happened on the cross, but the cross is offensive to us as well. It offends our sensibilities in every possible way. It is brutally, viscerally ugly, repugnant and without a trace of beauty. The cross is death in the raw, without any veneer of civilization or pretense of decency. It was designed to show the utmost contempt for its victims.

The Romans would never have crucified one of their own citizens – it was far beneath the dignity of even the basest of their own criminals. It was a death reserved for a subjugated people to demonstrate the total power, control, and unflinching authority of the Empire over the conquered peoples. Crucifixion was a raw warning to any who might dare challenge Rome.

Crucifixion stripped away every shred of human dignity from its victims. The crucifixion of Christ went beyond even the extreme norms of this most barbaric form of ancient execution. He was beaten almost beyond recognition, with His back ripped open by a vicious whipping that would've killed a lesser man. He was spat upon, abused verbally, stripped of all clothing, and a crown of thorns was beaten down into His scalp. His beard was ripped out by the handful. Huge spikes were driven through His wrists and feet. Finally, He was hung before the on-looking crowd who jeered and mocked Him as He faced the wrath due to our sin under a hot Mediterranean sun.

This was the death ordained for the Son of God as He bore our sin. It was offensive to every sensibility of anybody with even a shred of human compassion.

However, I think if we're honest with ourselves, we may find that much of our natural indignation at the cross is not out of sympathy for Jesus. Rather, it's because of what the message of the cross reveals about us. Jesus Himself was very clear about this – it was not His cross, but ours. This wasn't what He deserved, but what we deserved.

That offends our inherent pride and self-image. We like to tell ourselves that we're not so very bad. In fact, we're mostly good. We've tried, and if we've fallen a little short of perfection, well, we're only human. No one among us deserves to be treated to anything at all like the cross.

If we bristle when anyone points out the least character defect in us, how much more are we outraged at the concept that our sin is so bad that the cross was necessary? It's beyond all humanistic reason and flies

ESSENTIAL GRACE

in the face of our carefully constructed conception of ourselves.

In the flesh, we all feel that somehow, we deserve more dignity, more respect, more adulation and attention than we've received. It's an unusual person who can rise to prominence and respect in the world without betraying at least some sense of entitlement.

The pride of life is something to which we're all subject and is deeply ingrained in our nature. If we are already royalty, that's as it should be. If not, we imagine ourselves as the prince in frog's clothing, awaiting the enchanted kiss to restore our rightful glory. Pinning us to a cross is out of the question. We deserve glory, not shame. This we tell ourselves in the vanity of our own meditations. Truly humble and meek people are a rarity in this world.

Only grace can break through the horrible veneer of pride that afflicts us, and it takes the fullness of God's grace to bring about the complete transformation of humanity that is His ultimate aim.

I'd be remiss if I failed to point out how difficult this is for us. Yes, God gives all the grace we need to put to death the sins of the ego that are so deeply woven into our nature. Yet because it's accomplished by grace and not by our own works doesn't mean it's easy. Indeed, it's deeply painful. We must continually put the old man to death, and it tears at the core of our being to do so. Grace is not a divine anesthetic. It is divine enablement. Yet by grace, we must take up our cross if we're to follow Christ. That's the hardest decision you'll ever make as a Christian, and all of us resist it.[5]

That man's natural tendency is to resist the grace of God rather than embrace it highlights the absolute necessity of reconciliation. In our natural state, we're simply at odds with God. In fact, when pressed we find that people are openly hostile towards God and His revealed truth. The natural predisposition of mankind is to be at enmity with God.

Jesus didn't lay down His life just for His friends. He laid it down even for those of the race of Adam who remain His sworn enemies. The grace of this singular act was absolute. By Himself, He entered into the great aloneness of death, freely yielding His infinite and eternal life. He poured out the full sum necessary to reconcile the entirety of His fallen creation to Himself.

It's on the basis of the cross that all things will be judged and set right. The shadow of the cross is long, affecting all that is seen and unseen. None can escape

---

[5] There's much more to be said on this topic. Because he says it so much better than I ever could, I recommend to you *The Pursuit of God* by A.W. Tozer.

ESSENTIAL GRACE

its claims. It is the ultimate statement of redemption, ownership, and restorative intent towards His creation.

As Jesus proclaimed from the cross, redemption's power has been unleashed and does indeed "stand completed." Nothing can be added to the price that was paid and nothing can be taken away from it. This redeeming transaction is the sole basis on which all things will be reconciled.

Christ's sacrificial death on the cross perfectly satisfies God's justice and righteousness for all who accept it. It is powerful and complete, and it is available to all. Once accepted, our sin is fully accounted for and paid in full. The Spirit proclaims this truth through Paul:

"And you, being dead in your trespasses and the uncircumcision of your flesh, He has made alive together with Him, having forgiven you all trespasses, having wiped out the handwriting of requirements that was against us, which was contrary to us. And He has taken it out of the way, having nailed it to the cross" (Colossians 2:13-14).

The grace of reconciliation allows us to enter into the true rest, the Sabbath of God spoken of in the book of Hebrews. After the deep agony that brings reconciliation comes the even deeper peace of resting in God.

"There remains therefore a rest for the people of God. For he who has entered His rest has himself also ceased from his works as God [did] from His" (Hebrews 4:9-10).

It's from this place of rest that our work and service must begin, in the unshakeable confidence of knowing that we're forgiven, loved, redeemed, and restored into the fullness of God's love and favor. It is a service of grace. It's the ministry of reconciliation. The Holy Spirit works in us and through us. By grace, we become the ambassadors of reconciliation to our Lord's estranged creation.

What a marvelous privilege and responsibility this ministry is! Yet it's completely beyond our feeble abilities to perform. Reconciliation is the work of God, of the Father, of the Spirit, and of the Son. Nevertheless, we're not to fear to attempt it, so long as we rest in the great power of His enabling grace.

We *are* insufficient to the task, but as Paul said, we *"can do all things through Christ, who strengthens"* us. His power makes the ministry of reconciliation possible, and we must rely fully on His divine enablement. Paul lays it out for us:

ESSENTIAL GRACE

"Now all things [are] of God, who has reconciled us to Himself through Jesus Christ, and has given us the ministry of reconciliation, that is, that God was in Christ reconciling the world to Himself, not imputing their trespasses to them, and has committed to us the word of reconciliation. Now then, we are ambassadors for Christ, as though God were pleading through us: we implore [you] on Christ's behalf, be reconciled to God. For He made Him who knew no sin [to be] sin for us, that we might become the righteousness of God in Him," (2 Corinthians 5:18-21).

This is the great mission of God for His redeemed people. We're to carry the message of reconciliation to the world. This is one of the primary reasons that Jesus has left us here. All of the heartache and suffering that we may endure in His service is well worth even one lost child of Adam being reconciled to God eternally. It's primarily for this great ministry, and not at all for the fulfillment of our selfish desires, that we're granted full access to the grace of God and before the throne of Jesus Christ:

"Let us therefore come boldly unto the throne of grace, that we may obtain mercy, and find grace to help in time of need," (Hebrews 4:16).

DAVID M. DAMIANO

Our need and that of the world is truly great. We are in constant need of the enabling power of God's grace, and it is providentially available to us in unlimited supply. We are to seek it with all our heart. We must, for grace effects the reconciliation and transformation of man. Reconciliation and transformation are central to Jesus Christ's mission. The world desperately needs to hear of the grace of our Lord Jesus, and to see grace in action. We are called and enabled by grace to play our part in that great mission.

5 TRANSFORMATION

Free of all physical and spiritual agony, Jesus released Himself from the limitations of His human body into the infinite realm in which He had always dwelt. And yet it was different now, strange and alien after the immediacy of dwelling in the physical, though in the scope of eternity it had been but a moment.

He looked down on the scene. He knew the fear and bewilderment of the centurion, and the grief, despair and shock of John, Mary, and others among His dear friends.

Jesus beheld the resolve and boldness of Joseph of Arimethea and Nicodemus as they petitioned Pilate to *release His body to them, and their haste as they placed the body in the nearby garden tomb and sealed it with a great stone. He observed the vain posting of yet another Roman guard detachment to watch the grave, and the angels who stood a far more effective and powerful watch over the same, yet who were unseen by the human onlookers.*

At last, He watched the gathering shadows as the sun set on this strangest of all days. He was in it, but apart from it. In His soul, He longed to be in their midst again, to comfort, encourage, give a gentle touch, to explain, to feel with them, to share in their experience.

It was all novel and unprecedented; unexplored territory that yielded a perspective that He had anticipated, but which still moved Him deeply. He had not known what He would feel when it was time to make the great transformation, whether there would be any hesitancy.

Instead, and to His delight, there was rather a feeling of eagerness and keen desire. Were He of an impatient temper, He would have wished to get on with it this very instant, but He knew how to possess His desire in patience. The moment was soon, just a few spins of the earth on its axis and the time would be full, and everything would change forever, never to revert to how it had always been.

ESSENTIAL GRACE

He was glad He had work to do in the meanwhile. He went to it, knowing He was fully prepared for the greatest transformation that He would ever experience, a moment of such cosmic significance that it was impossible for even His closest followers and dearest friends to conceive its import.

On the dawn of the third day, the time was full. Of His death, He had left no doubt among either His followers or His enemies. Even the most scrupulous scribe must be satisfied that He had long departed that body which He had left behind on the cross and which was sealed in the tomb, now irretrievably dead, gone to the place of the dead. He had indeed gone to the place of the departed spirits, but He had returned, summoned by His Father, and moved by His Spirit.

*His conception may have seemed to man and angel like total commitment, His sacrificial and atoning death the ultimate expression of His infinite love and mercy, but He knew that **now** was the true point of no return, the moment when His commitment to humanity became absolute and eternal. He again followed the leading of the Spirit, much as He had at His incarnation. Only now, He moved the more consciously, with purposeful power and intent in the fullness of His own knowledge and will and desire, the Godhead in perfect harmony in the Son's glorious Being.*

The blackness of the tomb fled, overcome with a brilliant light which would have blinded the eyes of mortal man. It was so intense that it even flashed for a moment through the virtually impenetrable stone over the entrance, shocking the Roman guards into alertness. Divine light emanated from the body lying on the rocky shelf as the Spirit transformed it into a perfected and holy vessel, suited to the eternal habitation of the Almighty God.

It was the same substance, and yet marvelously transfigured, and into that formerly broken body, Jesus now entered, filling it with the infinite presence of His Eternal Life. He drew a mighty breath and sat up, unbinding Himself, even His raiment transformed and glorious.

He laughed out loud and shouted with joy. God had become Man, now and forever. The watching angels listened, marveling as the Father spoke to Jesus,

"You are my beloved Son; this day I have begotten You."

The angels rolled the stone away at His command, and the Roman guards fled in terror as His light burst forth, more intense and pure than the rising Mediterranean sun in the east.

Jesus strode out of the tomb; alive, incorruptible, eternal, immortal, the fullness of the Godhead dwelling bodily, a Man, One with His creation forevermore, God transformed, Man perfected. Nothing could ever be the same.

I remember very clearly the moment the Spirit first revealed the importance of the resurrection of Jesus Christ to me personally.

As a young man, I'd gone off course, straying from the things I had been taught and raised to believe as a child. Without realizing what was going on in my soul, I searched for spiritual answers and fulfillment, but in all of the wrong places.

Mysticism had great appeal to me, but I didn't have the patience to seek the promised enlightenment through years of self-denial and meditation. Instead, I turned to a shortcut, using psychoactive drugs as a way to connect with the spiritual world.

It was a dangerous yet effective path, and I soon discovered that the spiritual realm was quite real, full of personal forces that were stronger than I'd imagined. Voices spoke to me, stroking my ego, promising me knowledge and power. All I had to do was surrender to them.

I wasn't crazy. I knew these voices weren't a trick of my mind. They were clearly distinct persons outside of me. Terrified, I recognized that something wasn't right. I was seeking peace not power, and certainly didn't desire possession by an evil presence. Time went by, and I had no idea where to turn. Finally, I found no other option than to call out to God to protect and deliver me. I didn't know Him, yet He answered my prayer with power. The demonic presences vanished immediately. Still, I was lost and alone and didn't know what to do next.

To me, the Catholicism in which I'd been raised was never anything more than an empty and formal religious exercise and had seldom touched my spirit.[6] I had no desire to go back to it. However, some people from the Baptist church across the street had visited me once and I still had the tract with the service times. It was a Saturday night. I promised God I would go to that church the next morning.

I flushed my drugs down the toilet, threw my paraphernalia in the dumpster outside my apartment and went to a late movie (*Back to the Future*, as I recall), mostly because I was afraid to be in my apartment alone and needed to get out.

---

[6] In saying this, I don't intend to disparage Catholicism. I'm thankful for the foundational truths that I learned as a child. They prepared me for the work that the Spirit ultimately performed in my life.

ESSENTIAL GRACE

I came home, set my alarm, and went to bed, sleeping better than I had in a long time. When the alarm went off, I found I was very sleepy, and said to myself, "I'm tired. I will go next week."

Immediately, a voice spoke to me, as clear as anything I've ever heard. Unlike the demonic voices, He was gentle, patient and kind, but totally serious as He said,

"David, if you don't go today, you are never going."

I knew it was God, but I certainly had never expected Him to speak to me like that. I also knew exactly what He was saying — I had a choice to make, and it was a choice with eternal consequences. It wasn't something I could put off, but it was my choice. There was no compulsion. One thing I've learned about the Holy Spirit is that He never forces us to do anything against our will. That said, He can be very persuasive!

Surprised and shocked into wakefulness, I jumped out of bed, showered, dressed, and went to church. To me it was strange, and so unlike any place I'd ever been. I'm sure the message must have been simple and clear. Even so, it went right over my head. However, I sensed the presence of God among those people, something I'd never known before in church.

DAVID M. DAMIANO

The next day, I bought a Bible and began to read the New Testament. Wednesday, I went to the midweek prayer service. Still being a Catholic at heart, I figured I'd better start doing something for God if I was going to avoid hell. Serving God by spreading the gospel (whatever that was) seemed like a good place to start, so Thursday evening I went to visitation. I was surprised that the whole church wasn't there!

Even with all this activity, I was still lost and a stranger to Christ. But He was drawing me closer and closer. One of the deacons asked if I would like to go with him. He didn't know me, so he asked if I knew what we were doing. By my answer, I'm sure he could tell I really didn't have a clue.

He probably thought I was just a doubting Christian and began to go through verses that give assurance of salvation. I was lost, and it was exactly what I needed to hear to lead me home. He showed me verse after verse, and finally came to the passage that changed my destiny forever:

"That if you confess with your mouth the Lord Jesus and believe in your heart that God has raised Him from the dead, you will be saved. For with the heart one believes unto righteousness, and with the mouth confession is made unto salvation," (Romans 10:9-10).

ESSENTIAL GRACE

It was as if a great light was suddenly flooding through my whole being. I believed! Immediately, I knew I'd found what I was seeking. That instant I was born of the Spirit. By His grace and power, I was a new creation.

As I discovered that night, the resurrection of Jesus Christ is indeed the centerpiece of the gospel. In fact, a heartfelt belief in the truth of His resurrection is the fundamental component of saving faith. And no wonder. It's the most amazing and unexpected transformation conceivable.

On its verity, the entire body of revealed truth hinges. If the resurrection is true, then the message of the Bible is also confirmed as true, for throughout it testifies of Jesus and His resurrection. If the bodily resurrection of Jesus is false, then the Bible is a lie, and the God revealed in its pages is nothing but a mirage and an empty dream.

So it is that the resurrection of Christ is continuously under attack, both by fallen man and by the personal powers of spiritual darkness who are behind the world's deep animosity towards God.

These spiritual attacks are so severe and persistent that they may sometimes shake the faith of even the most grounded believer. Yet our faith in Jesus Christ need fear no truth that might be found in this world.

It certainly doesn't need to fear the lies of Satan and man.

Don't be dismayed by your occasional doubts. It's natural and normal for us to struggle to place the marvelous complexity of this universe into the framework of our own understanding. That struggle is indicative only of the limitations of our finite minds, not of any flaw in God's revelation. It's not the strength of our own belief, but the faithfulness of God that ultimately determines the outcome. And God is ever faithful to His promises.

Even though the resurrection of Jesus Christ is among the best-attested facts of ancient history, it's rejected by a great many rational people. Generally, people reject because it is so far outside of their own limited experience and understanding. Such rejection is often expressed with great confidence and condescension.

Yet it's natural man's presumed sense of rationality that is incomplete and faulty, for no man is omniscient. There's much about God beyond our experience and observational capacity. We're finite beings dwelling in time and can't possibly know everything. Therefore, we must admit that man's testimony to the resurrection is no more proof positive of its truth than man's doubt is a sufficient refutation of it.

ESSENTIAL GRACE

But we don't rely solely or even primarily on the testimony of man. We have the testimony of the Spirit of God, both in His written word and in His personal witness to us. God is above nature and perfectly able to speak directly to the human heart. Those who know Him aren't ashamed to testify that He speaks to us in many ways, even though we know the world mocks and laughs at those who make such spiritual claims.

Natural man's rationale for unbelief aside, the real marvel of the resurrection of Jesus Christ is not that God might raise the dead. It's hardly surprising that the Creator Who called the universe into existence out of nothing and created the magnificently diverse and interlocking web of life found on earth should be capable of raising the dead.

Indeed, it would be most shocking if He neglected to do so. Nor is it surprising that the Lord of Life couldn't be bound by death and was fully capable of transforming and reanimating His own recently dead body and taking it up once more.

No, the real marvel of the resurrection of Christ is not that it happened, but that He *chose* it. This was a choice with profound eternal consequences for Him. The Infinite God, unbound and unrestricted in the infinite realm of eternity, chose to unite Himself permanently and eternally with His creation. God forever became a man. That is a staggering transformation. Jesus Christ has bound Himself to human form.

When we realize this, it explains much in Scripture that might otherwise be puzzling. It wasn't at Christ's conception in Mary's womb that the Father said, *"This day have I begotten thee."* Nor at Jesus' birth in Bethlehem did He proclaim, *"This day have I begotten thee."* But at the resurrection, the Father made this great proclamation (see *Acts 13:33)*.

The amazing transformation of Jesus Christ at His resurrection was the absolute and eternal moment when God fully committed Himself to mankind. God became a Man, One of us. The world denies this glorious and transformative reality because it can't stand to consider its consequences.

On the basis of Christ's resurrection, we have fellowship with God. This fellowship is founded on what we have in common with Him, not the least of which is our shared humanity. That's the essence of John's message in his first epistle:

"THAT which was from the beginning, which we have heard, which we have seen with our eyes, which we have looked upon, and our hands have handled, concerning the Word of life – the life was manifested, and we have seen, and bear witness, and declare to you that eternal life which was with the Father and was

manifested to us – that which we have seen and heard we declare to you, that you also may have fellowship with us; and truly our fellowship [is] with the Father and with His Son Jesus Christ," (1 John 1:1-3).

The most obvious (but by no means least consequential) transformation of the resurrection is the physical change that transpired as Jesus permanently took on human form. The glorified body that Jesus has inhabited ever since the moment of His resurrection (and will continue to inhabit through all of eternity) is of the same type that we shall also possess when we are resurrected. This body is vastly different in nature compared to the bodies we possess in time. Paul lays this out with extraordinary clarity and precision:

"So also [is] the resurrection of the dead. [The body] is sown in corruption, it is raised in incorruption. It is sown in dishonor, it is raised in glory. It is sown in weakness, it is raised in power. It is sown a natural body, it is raised a spiritual body. There is a natural body, and there is a spiritual body. And so it is written, The first man Adam became a living being. The last Adam [became] a life-giving spirit. However, the spiritual is not first, but the natural, and afterward the spiritual. The first man [was] of the earth, [made] of dust; the second Man [is] the Lord from heaven. As

[was] the [man] of dust, so also [are] those [who are made] of dust; and as [is] the heavenly [Man,] so also [are] those [who are] heavenly. And as we have borne the image of the [man] of dust, we shall also bear the image of the heavenly [Man]," (1 Corinthians 15:42-49).

The Spirit reveals the nature of the resurrection body through a series of contrasts. All are drawn around the analogy of sowing a seed. Dying itself, a seed brings forth a living plant far more complex, glorious, and beautiful than the seed itself ever was. Yet the resulting plant perfectly expresses the inherent potential that was always within the seed.

The core comparison is between the "natural body" that we occupy in time and the "spiritual body" that we will inhabit in eternity. The Greek word translated "natural" in the NKJV is an adjectival form of the Greek word for soul. A fuller translation might be

"There is a body suited to the exercise of the soul, and there is a body suited to the exercise of the spirit."

I know there are many people of good faith and sound scholarship that believe man is comprised of only two parts (the physical body and the immaterial soul/spirit). Others hold that man is a being comprised of three parts (body, soul, and spirit).

It's true that soul and spirit are often used interchangeably in Scripture to refer to the immaterial aspect of our nature. However, I believe passages such as this one and *Hebrews 4:12* draw a very meaningful and important distinction between the two. The spirit is clearly the highest aspect of our being. It is the element of our existence most closely expressing the divine nature.

Undoubtedly, I'm oversimplifying a complex topic. However, such simplification helps us avoid getting lost in words. My basic understanding of the soul is that it is the seat of the senses. Through our soul, we experience and interpret the natural world all around us. The soul also encompasses our natural reasoning and much of our emotions.

Our fleshly nature operates in the material, "natural" (i.e., soul-centric) body. We want to see, hear, feel, taste, touch and smell and it is in those senses that we trust. It's in the soul's experience and familiarity with our senses that we "know". This is our natural focus, because we occupy a soul-centric body inherited from the "man of the earth", Adam.

However, through the exercise of our senses and natural reason alone, we can never fully know God. Knowing God requires the exercise of our spirit, something our natural body is not well attuned to. The spirit is our higher nature, the seat of creativity, imagination, philosophy, intuition, and the exercise of faith. The spirit is able to comprehend and perceive the supernatural, which is otherwise beyond our senses.

Our resurrection body will be in perfect harmony with the spirit, allowing us to experience an elevated plane of existence. This new body will share the nature of our resurrected Savior, who is truly the eternal Lord from heaven.

Even though our natural body operates primarily in the realm of the soul, it can still function at some level in the spiritual dimension. Likewise, our resurrected body, though attuned to the spirit, will still function in the realm of the senses.

As the spirit is higher than the soul, our resurrection body will be greater than our natural body. Our natural body is prone to corruption and decay, while our spiritual body will be incorruptible and will never break down. Our current bodies are weak, easily broken. Our spiritual bodies will be marvelously powerful and indestructible. We will be able to look into the face of God and see Him as He is.

The resurrection body will be glorious, a vessel of light, capable of many things that are physically impossible with our natural body. Jesus walked through physical walls, and yet His resurrected body was quite tangible and solid. He ascended into the heavens and didn't require wings to do so. Contrary to popular imagery, we will not become angelic beings with great, white wings. We won't need them!

The resurrection will be a marvelous transformation, but our reborn spirit is already operating in the resurrection realm. Although we don't sense the spiritual as fully as we will after our bodily resurrection, our awareness can and should grow. As we grow in grace, our spirit increasingly acknowledges the Holy Spirit's presence and is able to discern His voice.

The physical transformation of the Lord Jesus was just the beginning of His transformative ministry. At His resurrection, Jesus Christ also began to pour forth His grace upon humanity in multiple forms and on a scale unprecedented in the history of His previous dealings with man.

First, the Holy Spirit came to indwell and empower His children. Concurrently, Jesus bestowed individual gifts of grace, uniquely fitted to each of us, enabling us for service.

Moreover, His grace was manifested through the formation and empowerment of the church. The church itself is a complex spiritual organism. It provides a platform and a repository for those gifts to function together so that the whole is greater than the sum of the parts.

Finally, His grace is made available through the direct access He's granted to every believer before His throne of grace. There in His presence, we find the help we need to enable us to meet the challenges and trials we face daily.

God's grace in this present age has profoundly altered the course of human history. In unending succession, grace has been transforming life after life, directed by the sovereign will of the Father. The grace of God is never bestowed blindly, randomly, or generically, but is given purposefully, intentionally, and individually. At heart, that purpose is always transformational.

Practically, how does grace operate in us to produce transformation? The key is found in a surprising place — the local assembly of God's people. For it is in the church that God has distributed grace-gifts, differing in kind and application, but harmonized and coordinated for maximum effect.

God works through the multi-faceted grace present in the many members of the church. He bestows grace to achieve the transformation He desires. Remember, it was in the assembled church on the day of Pentecost (shortly following Christ's resurrection) that the Spirit first came in great power and visible form. He came to enable His people to testify of Jesus Christ. To change them. To change the world.

ESSENTIAL GRACE

Sadly, the local church is a greatly neglected, misunderstood and under-appreciated institution, even among believers. When we disengage from it, the church is weakened, because the grace given to us is no longer in play. As more of its members fall out, the church suffers, becoming weak and tepid. This discourages the remainder. Discouragement tempts us to withdraw, because there seems no point in attending and becoming active in such a dull and uninspiring place. It's a depressing, downward spiral.

The Spirit warns us not to forsake the assembling of ourselves together. In coming together as the people of God, the fullness of His grace is manifested towards us, channeled through human vessels:

"But to each one of us grace was given according to the measure of Christ's gift. Therefore He says: When He ascended on high, He led captivity captive, and gave gifts to men," (Ephesians 4:7-8).

"For it is the God who commanded light to shine out of darkness, who has shone in our hearts to [give] the light of the knowledge of the glory of God in the face of Jesus Christ. But we have this treasure in earthen vessels, that the excellence of the power may be of God and not of us," (2 Corinthians 4:6-7).

DAVID M. DAMIANO

The Greek word typically used in the New Testament for spiritual gifts is *charismata*, from the root word for grace. Literally, these are gifts of grace. Indeed, every grace gift is given for ministry, for it is in service to others that grace is most fully, powerfully, and dynamically expressed.

Grace gifts are given with one end in view: the transformation into His image of all the people that will hear His voice and respond to Him in faith. These grace gifts are seldom dramatic. Often, we don't even notice their operation.

However, when we're in the presence and fellowship of fellow believers, these gifts are operative and will have their intended effect. Through the coordinated operation of these manifold gifts, the presence of Christ is manifested in the world. This has been true from the Spirit's coming at Pentecost down to the present hour.

To activate our grace gifts, we must keep our focus on the Lord Jesus Christ. This is true even if you are unaware of what your grace-gifts are. In my experience, it's common for believers to be somewhat confused regarding the nature of their gifts. Our grace-gifts are so much a part of us that we often overlook them and fail to recognize how special these graces truly are. Nevertheless, every child of God is gifted by grace.

ESSENTIAL GRACE

We should strive for our fellowship to be continually mindful of the presence of Jesus and His Spirit, always aiming to glorify, magnify, and testify of Him. Doing so will bring out the full and coordinated power of the grace that our Lord has put within every member.

The church operates in seeming simplicity. The true power of its grace is concealed even when fully operative. It's despised by a world that can't recognize and refuses to see the spiritual dynamic that's at play. While it's hardly surprising that the world doesn't understand the church or recognize the gifts of God's children, it's a great shame that *we* should be ignorant of these powerful and transformative truths.

Don't allow the world's mockery to discourage you. After all, the world didn't recognize our Lord Jesus when He walked among them. He was rejected in spite of the fact that His life and works demonstrated His divine nature very clearly. If they couldn't recognize Him in His perfection, it's no wonder that they misunderstand us when the flaws of our old nature remain all too evident.

The presence of our old nature conceals and overshadows the beauty of our new nature. However, grace calls us, not to confidence in ourselves, but to confidence in the enabling and transforming power of our God:

"Therefore the world does not know us, because it did not know Him," (1 John 3:1).

"But by the grace of God I am what I am, and His grace toward me was not in vain; but I labored more abundantly than they all, yet not I, but the grace of God [which was] with me," (1 Corinthians 15:10).

"And as we have borne the image of the [man] of dust, we shall also bear the image of the heavenly [Man]," (1 Corinthians 15:49).

The local church is a living spiritual entity composed of individual believers, each with a unique and critical role to play in the manifestation and expression of God's grace. However, the real power for transforming the world is not in the constituent parts, but in the unified functioning of the whole.

Paul uses the analogy of the human body to describe how the church is designed to function. It's an apt analogy. The human body is an incredibly complex, interdependent, and balanced living system. If even one small element of the body is missing or malfunctions, the whole body suffers and may even die. We do a great disservice to the grace of God when we neglect any of the members of this spiritual body.

ESSENTIAL GRACE

Just as damaging is when we overly exalt any one member. This is particularly a problem if we allow a cult of personality to develop. It's spiritually dangerous and unhealthy for any person to be given preeminence in the church. There is only One Who is preeminent, our Lord Jesus Christ, the Head and Sustainer of the church.

We'll likely be very surprised at how the Lord ultimately judges His people and their works. Great gifts are only rewarded if they're used with great faith and with the humble recognition that they are indeed gifts of God.

It's in the coordinated working of all the grace gifts under the direction of the Holy Spirit and our Lord Jesus that the full power of God's grace is unleashed. The church itself desperately needs this transformation if we're to have the impact on the world that God intends.

If the church is to be transformed, the individual children of God who make up the church must also be changed. God became like us in order to enable us to become like Him. By so doing, He completely altered and redirected our destiny. We must focus on that destiny by faith. Our actions follow our focus. To be spiritual, we must operate in the vision of faith.

The Spirit's transformative work of grace begins in the realm of our minds, at the center of our spirit.

This is the essence of repentance (*metanoia*, lit. "*change of mind*"). Repentance is the necessary point of embarkation for our spiritual journey of transformation. It's a complete change of mind towards God. Our repentance is the beginning of a new focus that brings everlasting satisfaction, for to be spiritually minded is life and peace.

The grace of God leads us to repentance. That same grace is the essential new dynamic working in us from the moment of our rebirth, enabling us to walk according to the power and direction of the Holy Spirit. Without repentance, we'll naturally follow the desires of the flesh and our fallen minds.

We can have great confidence in this hope and in the enabling power of His grace to make it a reality. After all, our transformation is at the center of God's creative purpose.

"Being confident of this very thing, that He who has begun a good work in you will complete [it] until the day of Jesus Christ;" (Philippians 1:6).

The pain of this present age is suffered only because of this great end goal: to bring forth the full manifestation of all the children of God, completely changed into His image.

ESSENTIAL GRACE

"For the earnest expectation of the creation eagerly waits for the revealing of the sons of God," (Romans 8:19).

This outcome is our destiny, and the grace of God will prevail to fully deliver, change, and perfect us.

"For whom He foreknew, He also predestined [to be] conformed to the image of His Son, that He might be the firstborn among many brethren," (Romans 8:29).

As the grace of God begins its work in our minds, the focal point of our life changes. We turn away from our temporal desires and towards the eternal destiny that Christ has prepared for us. It's a new focus of faith. We're looking for that which we can't yet see, but which is in fact more real than the creation we know through our physical senses. Our part is to choose what our minds will focus on. We must choose either our selfish, temporal desires, or the eternal, spiritual promises of God.

"And do not be conformed to this world, but be transformed by the renewing of your mind, that you may prove what [is] that good and acceptable and perfect will of God," (Romans 12:2).

"And be renewed in the spirit of your mind, and that you put on the new man which was created according to God, in true righteousness and holiness" (Ephesians 4:23-24).

The grace to make the right choice is freely available to all. Nevertheless, it's a continual struggle as we find our affections torn between two competing realities. Little wonder that we're sometimes confused about what we should be seeking from God.

I remember vividly a season of prayer many years ago. I struggled in vain to truly connect with God. When I finally got out of the way enough to find myself in His presence, the Lord spoke to me plainly,

"Ask whatever is in your heart David, and I will grant it."

I was startled and totally taken aback. After all that wrestling, I had no idea what to ask! All I could say was, "You know my heart, Lord. Let Your will be done."

Perhaps I wasted my once-in-a-lifetime opportunity and should have asked some great and wise thing. Or perhaps I got it just right. My sense in that moment was that I already had what I was seeking. There really wasn't much left to ask. Looking back, I stand by that. Knowing God is glory enough, which is very evident when we're actually confronted with His presence.

"Likewise the Spirit also helps in our weaknesses. For we do not know what we should pray for as we ought, but the Spirit Himself makes intercession for us with groanings which cannot be uttered. Now He who searches the hearts knows what the mind of the Spirit [is,] because He makes intercession for the saints according to [the will of] God," (Romans 8:26-27).

"That He would grant you, according to the riches of His glory, to be strengthened with might through His Spirit in the inner man, that Christ may dwell in your hearts through faith; that you, being rooted and grounded in love, may be able to comprehend with all the saints what [is] the width and length and depth and height–to know the love of Christ which passes knowledge; that you may be filled with all the fullness of God," (Ephesians 3:16-19).

The grace of God continually enables our transformation as the children of God. However, in the process it exposes many things about us that make us uncomfortable. Some of these things we may prefer not to know. Nevertheless, these are the very things we must acknowledge and allow to be purged if we're to be transformed.

Transformation begins with confession. Literally, our internal voice must willingly "speak the same thing" as the Spirit. Confession is nothing more or less than our mind coming into full recognition and active agreement with what the Spirit is revealing. The word of God is a mirror which shows us who we are and what we shall be. It's our guide to the practical working of grace in our lives.

"For the word of God [is] living and powerful, and sharper than any two-edged sword, piercing even to the division of soul and spirit, and of joints and marrow, and is a discerner of the thoughts and intents of the heart," (Hebrews 4:12).

"But we all, with unveiled face, beholding as in a mirror the glory of the Lord, are being transformed into the same image from glory to glory, just as by the Spirit of the Lord," (2 Corinthians 3:18).

Uncomfortable as this transformation into God's image may sometimes be, ultimately, it's liberating. As Jesus said,

ESSENTIAL GRACE

"And you shall know the truth, and the truth shall make you free," (John 8:32).

"But he who looks into the perfect law of liberty and continues [in it,] and is not a forgetful hearer but a doer of the work, this one will be blessed in what he does," (James 1:25).

The liberty we're given isn't the false freedom of licentiousness. That which the world calls liberation (i.e., the unashamed and selfish indulging of our lusts and desires) is a counterfeit. In fact, it's the self-imposed bondage to our own corruption and sin. This so-called "liberty" leads ultimately to death.

Rather, grace sets us free to be the people that God has intended and purposed from eternity past. It's a glorious liberty, breaking our chains of bondage and enabling us to soar into God's presence. In this great spiritual liberty, we may ascend to spiritual heights that our old nature couldn't even comprehend. As we do so, we fully experience the acceptance, love, and joy of our Lord.

In this liberty, we're empowered by the Spirit to fulfill our destiny, both in time and eternity. In time, we'll find the deep satisfaction of fulfilling the work that God, from eternity past, has ordained for us to carry out. In eternity, we'll experience the everlasting joy of being in the very presence of God and learning of Him forever.

The tremendous freedom of grace is due to the nature of grace itself. The enablement and power for this great transformation doesn't depend on us at all but comes complete from God. It's perfectly suited to our need at every step along the way.

Such grace is always sufficient to fulfill God's plans and purposes for us. That's the true liberty empowered by grace. The entire creation waits in anticipation for its complete manifestation.

"Now the Lord is the Spirit; and where the Spirit of the Lord [is], there [is] liberty," (2 Corinthians 3:17).

"Because the creation itself also will be delivered from the bondage of corruption into the glorious liberty of the children of God," (Romans 8:21).

By grace, we have no more need of the law. The spirit of life in Jesus Christ has truly made us free from the law of sin and death. We're never to go back into our failed efforts at following the law. We are to walk instead in the glorious liberty of the children of God, triumphant in the divinely enabling power of grace.

6 Consummation

When the end had finally arrived, it proved to Him far more difficult than the beginning. So many details to attend to; wrongs that must be set right, wounds that must be healed, debts that must be settled, justice that must be meted out, deeds of darkness that must be brought into the light.

He could not bring His creation to completion before every matter of every living soul, even the most seemingly trivial, was dealt with. No one must enter the eternal state without a full accounting that satisfied the understanding of God, man, and angel. All *must be reconciled with His perfect justice and righteousness.*

God had borne with humanity as long as He could, until it would have been unjust and pointless to wait any longer. The evil and unbelief and rebellion of mankind had reached its fullness, to the point where only judgment had been able to reach that remnant who might still be salvaged from the wreckage and destruction of sin. Sadly, in the end most had rebelled, even as they had faced the obviously supernatural judgments of God unleashed on the earth.

He had already raised every one of His redeemed people, from the first to the last, transforming their former bodies of clay and earthly substance into glorious bodies suited to their perfected spirits. They were raised in His own glorified image so that they could now look upon Him and see Him for the first time as He truly was and always had been. Infinite, perfect, holy, glorious, and beautiful beyond measure, as each of them were now also. All of His children stood before Him, incorruptible, eternal, and immortal.

And now at the very end, all the lost had finally also been raised bodily in a great, fearful and solemn assembly to stand before His throne, a vast sea of humanity that no man could number, spread out across a wide plain before His holy mount.

ESSENTIAL GRACE

It was noisy and raging and pulsing with fear, anger, sorrow, despair, confusion, anticipation. One by one, they were called to ascend the wide steps up the base of the mountain, drawn by an irresistible power, passing by the host of the redeemed, perhaps catching a confused glimpse of someone they had once known in another time, surprised to see them standing exalted and in glory.

Finally, each found himself before the Throne, bowing in the presence of the King of Kings, acknowledging His authority and Lordship over them. He dealt with each one personally and by name. There was no time in that place and there was no place to hide. They were totally exposed before His eyes. Their innermost being revealed and laid bare. It was forever, and it was but a moment.

For those who had refused His mercy, the punishment matched the offense at every point. Many who had knowingly and proudly rebelled against God and all He stood for now quaked and wept before Him. Even these received less from His hand than they would have dealt out were their positions reversed.

However, His greatest compassion was reserved for those who had been the most ignorant, and He wept with them as they were consigned to their fate. It was painful and distressing beyond all reckoning, for even in His consuming wrath, He was filled with mercy and love and the desire to forgive what could no longer be forgiven.

Imperceptibly at first, the great tide of humanity from all the ages of the earth slowly receded, lost to His presence forevermore, as each received their due. Finally, the last fallen son of Adam had been dealt with and departed, the vast plain was empty, and the still nearly innumerable company of His elect angels and His redeemed children stood with Him on the great mountain.

There was a profound silence. There were tears in every eye. It was done. Never to be undone. The great sea of lost humanity was departed and was no more. Only one thing remained, and that was to forget. Perhaps that was the hardest part. So much that might have been, and now would never be ... and yet, forget He must, that He might bring His beloved into eternal joy.

As they looked out over the empty plain, all assembled now saw that it was in fact the whole of the universe beneath the mountain. It was splendid in its detail, depth, and scope. There were millions of galaxies and uncountable stars, objects of wonder and untold beauty, most of it never before seen by the eyes of man, and yet from their current vantage they could see it all at once as if it were a very small thing.

ESSENTIAL GRACE

They marveled as they beheld it, as if for the first time seeing that even this grandeur was a mere fringe of the garment of His glory. They listened to the silence and found that it was alive with a deep thrumming song of the measureless and almost timeless depths of space.

And just as they began to comprehend, Jesus spoke to His creation.

"Your purpose is fulfilled. Through great travail, you have brought forth the children of the living God! Well done! Depart now and let all of your labors and chaos cease."

At His word of command, the whole of that vast and incredible universe flashed into brilliant light, and just as suddenly collapsed into a singularity and vanished into an outer blackness that itself blinked out of existence without a trace to be seen or heard, fleeing from before His throne, departing in silence from the glory of His presence.

The world that once was left neither echo nor shadow. There was no smoke, or vapor, or lingering odor, or flickering light. Instead, there was only a great silence and emptiness spread out across the infinite expanse.

All were focused on the One who sat on His white throne, there upon the immensity of the eternal mountain of Zion, suspended in the Light Which Had Always Been. Each of His redeemed were also standing arrayed in their places below Him, unmovable and waiting, barely breathing, the atmosphere heavy and still.

Jesus stood up from the throne, and every one of His children felt His immediate presence before them as He spoke.

"The time for tears is gone ... peace ... peace ... be still. There is nothing done that may be undone, no regret that has not been set right. Your sorrows are past, your fears are no more, your cares are lifted, and you are greatly loved. Rest now, and sorrow no more forever."

At His word there was a collective sigh, as the release of a repressed sob. And Jesus waited, and kept His counsel and joy in His own heart.

Each one was absorbed in their thoughts and meditations, in a silence and stillness that could never be fully told.

And then one in the midst began to sing, slowly and softly at first, then stronger as other voices began

ESSENTIAL GRACE

to rise, until every voice had joined the spontaneous song of praise.

It was sweeter than any song that had ever been heard in heaven or earth, and they all knew every word. And everyone knew their part, even though it was a new song in a new key and a new tongue. The great chorus rolled as an almost physical presence over the One who stood before the throne.

How long they sang no one could tell, for they were outside of time. But there were millions upon millions of verses so that all who sang told their personal redemption story. Each voiced their own worship of the Son, with every life story entwined with that of numerous others in marvelous and unexpected complexity. It was a multidimensional composition of life expressed in music sublime.

Jesus heard every shading and detail without missing the perfect harmony of the whole. Only His own infinite soul could know the fullness of joy that He felt as He took it in.

The song came down from its mighty crescendo, voices dropping out gradually until the first voice was left to finish alone, just as it had begun.

Jesus smiled, and it was like the first warm sun of spring after a long winter, and everyone felt that His smile was just for them, for so it was.

DAVID M. DAMIANO

"Come, we must go higher."

He turned and began to ascend the great peak with its top hundreds of miles above, hidden by the mountain's massive shoulders and lesser summits, from which the true summit could almost, but not quite, be glimpsed. As one, the great assembly followed Jesus ever higher around and around the mountain's flanks.

As they climbed, Jesus Himself began to sing, but His song was of a harmony that only His own voice, greater than the sound of many waters, could carry, with words that only He could know, a song of new creation, of new heavens and a new earth.

With every melodic word, fresh marvels appeared all around them. Some were familiar and yet subtly altered, strangely transfigured, improved and glorified so that they were no longer base, but now perfectly fitted to this new and higher reality. Others were so novel that they could never have been imagined in that former time and place. And though never before seen or heard, everything was somehow familiar and fitting and just right.

There was laughter and shouts of joy, as here a beloved family pet leapt to join its master's side, different and yet unmistakably himself. Meanwhile, way out beyond them, one of the assembly glimpsed a golden rolling countryside that looked better than it had ever

ESSENTIAL GRACE

looked when once they had called its distant shadow "home", a word which had never carried fuller meaning than at that moment.

As they went, the company had swelled to include so many delightful creatures walking and swimming and flying in their midst that it would seem the mountain could not hold them all, and yet it did, for it was also growing and changing, transformed and transfigured as Jesus sang.

Each revelation brought forth expressions of wonder and joy, and every single member of that mighty company had more to see and hear and experience than they could possibly take in, so that they were constantly looking about as one of their companions pointed out something of special interest to them.

Seemingly, there was nothing good, nothing that had once brought joy, nothing that had ever been lost and missed, but was now found again. Only now, it was perfected and restored, to the deep satisfaction of their overflowing souls.

So marvelous and refreshing was the experience, so varied and deep the wonders that they shared, that finally it seemed that there may never have been anything else, that they had always been climbing that mountain and following their Savior, experiencing His joys and watching Him create. Perhaps they had been, and the rest had been but a shadow and a dream?

They had entered the true reality. Here, the light and substance could never fade or be diminished. Every sadness and grief and pain were so distant that it might never have been, and though they felt they had been climbing forever, yet none was tired, for all were eternally young and vibrant. Every step only increased their strength and sense of well-being and peace.

At length, and yet in no time at all, they found themselves on the summit. It was not the small and glimmering point they had sensed from below, but was indeed broad and flat, smooth as a sea of glass, crystalline and luminescent, immeasurable and yet transparent so that they could see right through the mountain and once again view all of creation spread out beneath and around them.

Only now, it was the new creation. It was far more beautiful and intimate than before; warm and immediate instead of distant, cold, and daunting as the former. Yet it was also vaster and more varied, so that they gazed and listened in even greater wonder and joy than before. All of it was lit to even the greatest depth by the presence of Jesus standing at its center.

Each soon discovered that if they looked with desire at any portion of it, they found themselves at that very spot, fully immersed and present in it, and yet strangely still present with Jesus and their gathered brethren on the summit at the same instant.

ESSENTIAL GRACE

It was a novel experience which quickly became quite normal, as they moved wherever their spirit willed, at the speed of thought and yet without any effort whatsoever. They were seemingly everywhere at once, so that there was no rush or urgency to see anything, and they explored only for joy and the praise of their Lord.

There was not a hastened word from Jesus or anyone else to either disturb their reverie or hinder their fellowship, for it was the long and flowing eternal Now in which they dwelt, without the pressure and movement of time to intrude on even the least of their enjoyment. And often and unexpectedly they found Jesus right beside them, and no joy could match that of His presence.

Every spirit was overflowing, and no matter how much they drank in of this new place, there was always room for more and always something new that they had never noticed before. And in every heart was the singing recognition of Home. Yet they did not know they were still only on the threshold.

They were not aware of any voice calling their attention, but all felt their gaze drawn upward to the illuminated vastness above, to an expanse filled with stars more brilliant and beautiful than any ever seen in the former world.

But one in particular drew the eye, its light coming from what seemed to all to be the north. It was more spectacular than the rest, growing in luster and depth, imperceptibly at first but now quite obviously descending to them, coming into sharper and clearer focus like a multi-faceted gem that seemed to carry the beauty of everything they had ever witnessed or known up to that moment and yet exceeding even the extent of that greatest sum.

As it drew ever nearer, they could see it was roughly of a great pyramidal shape, its base was four-square and its pinnacle the same height as its width and depth, ten million times more massive than any mountain of the old and vanished world, greater even than the eternal mountain of Zion on which they stood.

It was not a city of the plains or mountains, but rather a mountain of a city, with no appearance of artifice. Indeed, it was almost organic and alive, as if even its deepest core were comprised of living stones, each branching from and connected to the Stone cut out without hands at its heart.

Far from symmetrical in the geometric sense, its towering form beyond the well-ordered base was nonetheless suffused with the sensibility of great purpose and creativity while fully retaining the majesty of pristine wilderness that was inherent to its perfect balance and harmony.

ESSENTIAL GRACE

It was the wildest and yet most civilized thing that the great assembly would ever see. But nothing was out of place or chaotic in all of its streets and gardens, paths and forests, valleys and hills, all nourished and connected by a river flowing, sometimes in great cascades and cataracts but often in still and deep pools through peaceful valleys. Ever down the river flowed from the highest reaches of the City.

Undergirding it was a strong foundation of twelve distinct layers, each a singular and magnificent gem, diverse in kind but each an integral part of the whole. No one needed to be told the names of the foundations, for they were the names of their honored brothers who had walked with Jesus and were now with them; the very apostles who had carried His message to every kindred and nation and tribe from which most of the great assembly had sprung.

And they knew the names on the twelve gleaming gates of pearl, three to a side, for those were the names of Israel's sons, and both the father and those very sons were also in their midst along with a great company of the children of Abraham and of the patriarchs who had come before him.

And as they looked, they knew that each of their names were also written throughout in the stones and paths of the City. Some recorded in places great and prominent and some on the lesser eminences, but each glorious and fitly placed. Not one stone was missing, and it would not have been complete and whole without any of them.

The sight of it was a cause of joy to every heart, but most especially to the heart of Jesus. This was at last and indeed the heavenly city, New Jerusalem, the place of promise that had drawn them and whose hope had sustained their spirits in the lowest hours of their temporal pilgrimages, more beautiful and perfect than they had ever imagined.

Spiritually, it was their mother and their home, the dwelling place of God, a place of harmony, peace, and rest from which they could enjoy eternity as they dwelt in perfect fellowship with each other and with their God. And it was now ready and awaiting the much-anticipated reception of its King, its children, and its angelic inhabitants. For what is a city without a people to dwell in it? And once populated with the great company of the redeemed, it was indeed the Bride, the Lamb's Wife.

At a nod from Jesus, angels began sounding trumpets, festive and lilting until the whole of the new creation rang with their sound, and then one of the angels lifted up his voice so that all could hear.

"Open, ye everlasting gates, and be lifted up, that the King of Glory may come in."

ESSENTIAL GRACE

At once, all twelve of the massive pearly gates opened, never to be closed again, and a sweet fragrance of the purest atmosphere gently flowed over the great assembly as if the very breath of God.

The whole company began to form a great procession of twelve columns, one under each banner of the twelve tribes of Israel. Every person knew his place without needing to be told, and the Lord Jesus was at the head of the tribe of Judah, riding His magnificent white horse, the King of Kings returning victorious from battle great and perilous. Every one of the children of the King likewise found themselves mounted and ready to enter the Celestial City.

There were no visible paths, roads, or staircases to any of the gates of the City as it hovered in space above them. So of course, they must fly, which did not seem a strange thing at all after the wonders they had already experienced. It was apparently more natural for these horses than walking or running.

He led the way, and they circled the mighty wall so that all could see it from every angle. There had never been a carousel or amusement ride to rival this, but no one was terrified of the dizzying heights ascended. It was pure exhilaration and anticipation.

Each contingent entered in their appointed order, Jesus preceding them all by a regal, but not great, distance. And as each entered, the angel of the gate *greeted and welcomed them by name; none were addressed by their old names, but with new names that suited them perfectly.*

And many that one would have thought might come first instead came last. And some that the world had esteemed least came first. But all were exactly where they should be. And it was all so perfectly just and right, that none would have complained even if some vestige of their former sinful selves had been left to do so, which was not the case, for sin and selfishness and pride had been banished and purged forever and could never enter that new and glorified state.

The road to the summit was long, but the company was so great that, as the last were entering the gates, the Lord Jesus was just reaching the top of the City, and like Zion it was found to have a great open space sufficient for them all.

Somewhere along the way they had dismounted and now walked, their steeds finding their own paths back to their places without the need for any steward or groom, for they possessed a nobility and intelligence of their own, as did all the creatures of that place.

And as they came to the top, they found that there were beautiful pavilions set on the broad lawn, with tables and a great feast spread, everyone with a place and no spot left vacant.

ESSENTIAL GRACE

In the midst stood Jesus, His light suffusing the whole city, and from His new throne a great fountain of the water of life poured forth, the very source of the river they had marveled at as they wound their way upward. And on both banks of the river, the tree of life grew, with its twelve different types of fruit, and no tree they had ever seen could match it for beauty, vitality, and wholesomeness.

The same angel who had called for the gates to open spoke once more.

"Now is come the marriage supper of the Lamb; greatly blessed are all who have been called."

And as they looked around, they realized that they were the City and the City was the Bride, and that this was the Great Assembly, the manifold grace of God embodied in glorified humanity, and that they were together become the temple of the Living and Everlasting God.

Jesus raised a cup for His Bride, and all joined in.

Then to the great delight of Himself and His children, Jesus passed through the whole host of the assembly, serving each and every one personally with a word of kindness and praise, and there was not one who did not receive His presence with wonder, amazement, satisfaction and deep humility, for such grace as His was beyond compare.

How long they celebrated together no one could tell, for there were delights and joys without measure as they freely came and went, mingling throughout the great multitude. God was truly All and in all, and they marveled and learned continually of His inexhaustible glory forevermore in that new world without end ...

And God was never alone again.

ABOUT THE AUTHOR

David became a follower of Christ in 1985, and received a Master of Divinity degree from Baptist Bible Graduate School of Theology in 1991. He has served in a variety of pastoral and teaching ministries since then.

David and his wife have two grown children. They divide their time between North Idaho and the Oregon Coast, surrounded by the beauty and majesty of God's creation.

www.ingramcontent.com/pod-product-compliance
Lightning Source LLC
Chambersburg PA
CBHW020544030426
42337CB00013B/977